Together Yet Apart

A Partner's Guide to Relationship OCD – Supporting your loved one without losing yourself

By

Tracy Foster

MAPLE
PUBLISHERS

Disclaimer

The information in this book is general guidance about the subject matter and not a person's specific individual circumstances. Neither is it a substitute for medical or alternative professional advice on specific or personal circumstances. Please consult your medical practitioner or other health care professional if you are experiencing distress that may require additional intervention. As far as the author is aware, the information given is accurate and up to date. The author does not assume responsibility for omissions, alternative interpretations or errors on the subject matter. The author disclaims, as far as UK law allows, any liability arising directly or indirectly from the use or misuse of the information contained in this publication.

Acknowledgements

It is important for me to express my heartfelt thanks to Laura Heavens-Gove, owner of HG Virtual Business Services, for the dedication, creativity and compassion she has brought to my OCD and ROCD awareness work through social media. Her ability to translate complex emotional experiences into accessible, meaningful content has supported so many people who struggle silently. The conversations sparked and lived experiences shared through my social media platforms have informed and enriched some of the ideas within this book. I am grateful for her insight, professionalism and commitment to raising awareness, and for the energy and care she brings to my growing business and her own.

ISBNs
978-1-80723-076-0 (Paperback)
978-1-80723-077-7 (Hardback)
978-1-80723-078-4 (E-Book)

Connect with Author:
tracy.foster_counsellingservices@hotmail.co.uk
www.rocdtracyfoster.com

Book Layout and Cover Design by:
Maple Publishers
www.maplepublishers.com

Book Illustrations by: Sarah Colbert, Graphic Designer

Published by:
Maple Publishers
Fairbourne Drive, Atterbury,
Milton Keynes,
MK10 9RG, UK
www.maplepublishers.com

A CIP catalogue record for this title is available from the British Library.

CONTENTS

Preface and Introduction

I wrote my first book, 'ROCD: *Is It a Thing?*', after supporting people with Relationship OCD for over a decade.

I hoped to shed light on an experience that many people silently endure – the confusion, guilt and emotional turmoil of Relationship OCD (ROCD). I wanted to give those suffering with intrusive doubts about their relationships a sense of understanding, normalcy, hope and self-guidance.

OCD sufferers from around the world have shared their experiences with me. They finally felt heard and understood, and realised that, through their experiences, they were not alone. Unsurprisingly, through continued awareness, what has been interesting is that, among these voices, another group began to emerge: those who weren't necessarily struggling with ROCD themselves but were deeply affected by someone who was.

Partners, parents, friends, and spouses have reached out to me describing the weight they are carrying, the emotional confusion of trying to support a loved one caught in obsessive thoughts, the helplessness of being unable to "fix" what is happening and the quiet erosion of their own self-esteem as they become entwined in the cycle of reassurance seeking from their loved one and the subsequent doubt that it brings.

Some share how they question their own worth or behaviour, wondering if they have somehow caused intrusive thoughts or anxiety. Others admit to feeling guilty about their frustration, resentment, exhaustion, or even anger. Many say, "I love them, but I don't know how to help, or how to cope anymore. ROCD sufferers also share their partners' frustrations with me, which only served to increase their own guilt.

It has become increasingly clear to me that while there is growing awareness of OCD and one of its subsets, Relationship OCD, there remains very little understanding of the ripple effect it creates for those who love and care for the person experiencing it. These carers often suffer in silence, emotionally worn down, unsure where to turn, and afraid to speak openly about their own distress for fear of seeming unsupportive or causing further upset.

I have written this book to fill that gap.

As a counsellor, I see, first hand, the toll that ROCD can take on relationships, not only romantic ones, but also between parents and children, friends, and even within families. My work also shows that carers need a voice, validation and practical strategies just as much as the person experiencing OCD does.

My intention with this book is to offer both understanding and guidance to:

- Explain how ROCD works and why it can feel so personal when it isn't.
- Show how carers can offer support without losing themselves in the process.
- Help rebuild self-worth, confidence and emotional boundaries.
- Create empathy on both sides, because healing a relationship touched by ROCD involves compassion for everyone involved.

If you are reading this as someone who loves a person with ROCD, please know that your pain is real, your exhaustion is valid, and your feelings deserve space. Supporting someone through OCD can be immensely challenging, but you are not powerless. With insight and communication, both of you can rediscover balance and understanding.

My first book spoke to those directly affected by ROCD. This one is written for you - the partner, the friend, the parent, the carer - who wants to help but also needs to heal. I hope this will give you both the reassurance and the permission to take care of yourself as well.

Tracy Foster

Counsellor/Cognitive Behaviour Therapist (Reg MBACP)

Author of “ROCD, *Is it a thing*?”

How to use this book

Like "ROCD, *Is it a thing?*", this book is designed as both a guide and a companion, something you can return to at different stages of your journey as a carer, partner or loved one of someone living with Relationship OCD (ROCD). It is not meant to be read in one sitting or approached as a rigid programme. Instead, think of it as a series of conversations, a space to pause, reflect and learn in your own time.

You might find some chapters deeply relatable and comforting, while some chapters may bring about some difficult emotions to sit with. That's okay. Healing and understanding are not linear processes. Permit yourself to step away when needed, to breathe, and to return when you feel ready.

While this book focuses primarily on the partner's perspective, it can also open up meaningful discussions between you and your loved one. Some sections are written with shared reflection in mind, helping you both explore experiences with compassion and curiosity rather than blame or defence.

If your partner is working through "ROCD, *Is it a thing*?", the two books can complement each other beautifully – one offering insight from the inside out, and the other from the outside in.

As in my 1:1 counselling work, I want to emphasise that each person's situation is unique. You can experience ROCD in the context of a romantic relationship, a family relationship, a close friendship, or any meaningful connection, or you may be supporting someone who is. You might be a partner, a parent of an adult child, or someone navigating ROCD in a different relational setting altogether. You might live together, live apart, or have limited contact. The principles outlined in these pages are intended to be flexible and adaptable to your specific context. Take what resonates and leave what doesn't.

Throughout this book, you'll find practical tools, insights and gentle guidance tailored to the unique challenges of supporting someone with ROCD. These are designed to help you:

- Understand the dynamics of ROCD more clearly.
- Recognise your own emotional responses.
- Build healthier boundaries and communication patterns.
- Restore your sense of self and wellbeing.

Alongside the core strategies, I offer a selection of "out of the box" (lesser-known) ideas and techniques for you to experiment with. These are simple, grounding and sometimes unexpected approaches designed to help you navigate the emotional intensity, uncertainty, and fatigue that can come with caring for someone experiencing ROCD. Not every idea will be right for every situation; you don't have to complete every exercise; and there are no "right" answers. But by trying different techniques, you can discover what best supports you, strengthens your resilience, and helps you stay connected to yourself throughout the process.

Use them as opportunities and explore what feels right for you.

A comforting note

Supporting someone with ROCD can be emotionally draining, confusing and at times, isolating. This book isn't about blame, fixing or assigning responsibility. It's about understanding. It's about permitting you to care without losing yourself, and to offer empathy while still honouring your own needs.

No one is expected to do this perfectly, because perfection does not exist. You are learning, healing and doing your best – and that is more than enough.

A note on language and understanding

Before you begin, I want to explain that this book contains a glossary at the back.

If you are new to OCD, whether you are supporting someone with it, living with it yourself, or trying to understand it better, you may already have noticed how many psychological terms are used when OCD is discussed. Words like trigger, intrusive thoughts, reassurance, or rumination are often mentioned as though their meaning is obvious. Many of these words are misunderstood, used differently in everyday language, or carry a very specific meaning within OCD.

In recent years, psychological language has become more common in everyday life. This can be helpful, but it can also create confusion. People may feel they are supposed to understand these terms already or feel embarrassed to ask what they mean. Others may think they know a word because they have heard it used casually, without realising that in OCD it describes a very particular process. This can minimise the seriousness of the disorder, and for someone with OCD, this can feel invalidating, and they can feel very misunderstood. Their condition involves intense distress, not personality or character quirks. It can increase stigma and make sufferers less likely to feel seen or seek support.

Learning about OCD does not need to add another layer of difficulty to what is already an overwhelming condition. The purpose of the glossary is not to be academic or technical, but to offer clear, plain-language explanations that make what you are reading easier to follow.

You don't have to remember every definition or read the glossary from start to finish. It is simply there as a reference point that you can return to if a word feels unclear, confusing or loaded.

Language matters, and the right words can bring understanding and help you make sense of an OCD sufferer's experience, and not knowing the language yet is entirely normal.

Chapter 1

Understanding OCD

1.1 How OCD Develops

Obsessive-compulsive disorder (OCD) does not develop because someone is difficult, insecure, controlling, or unwilling to let things go. It is not a personality flaw, a lack of insight, or a failure of love or commitment. OCD is a mental health condition that arises from a complex interaction of biology, brain functioning, and life experience.

For partners and carers, understanding this provides an essential foundation. Without it, OCD-driven behaviours can easily be misread as intentional, meaningful, or relationally motivated, when, in reality, they are symptoms of a disorder that operates independently of values, intentions, and character.

1.2 The Brain and OCD

OCD is associated with differences in how particular brain circuits function, particularly those involved in threat detection, error monitoring, and uncertainty. In simple terms, the OCD brain is exceptionally good at noticing potential danger but struggles to switch off once that alarm has been triggered.

Neurochemicals such as serotonin play a role, which is why medication can be helpful for some people. However, OCD is not a simple chemical imbalance. It is better understood as a disorder of misfiring safety mechanisms: the brain repeatedly signals that something is wrong, incomplete, or unsafe, even when no real threat is present.

1.3 Genetics and vulnerability

OCD often runs in families. This does not mean that someone is destined to develop it, but it does mean that some people are born with a greater vulnerability. This can be thought of as a nervous system that is more sensitive to uncertainty, doubt, and perceived risk.

This vulnerability can remain dormant for years. Many people with OCD describe themselves as conscientious, responsible, empathetic, or deeply caring long before symptoms appear. These traits do not cause OCD, but OCD often attaches itself to what matters most to the person.

1.4 Stress, triggers, and onset

For many people, OCD symptoms emerge during periods of stress or transition. This might include adolescence, illness, loss, significant life changes, or increased responsibility. Stress does not cause OCD on its own, but it can activate underlying vulnerability.

Once OCD has been triggered, it does not require ongoing stress to continue. The disorder becomes self-sustaining through its internal logic and behavioural cycles.

1.5 The OCD cycle: Why it persists

At the heart of OCD is a powerful learning loop:

1. An intrusive thought, image, feeling, or doubt appears.
2. The brain interprets this as dangerous or significant.
3. Anxiety or distress rises.
4. A behaviour or mental action is used to reduce that distress.
5. Temporary relief occurs.
6. The brain learns that the behaviour was necessary.

Over time, this cycle strengthens. Compulsions, whether visible or mental, are not performed because the person believes the fear, but because they are trying to feel safe, certain, or at peace again.

This is why reassurance-seeking, checking, analysing, or avoidance may appear deliberate or repetitive to a partner, while feeling urgent and unavoidable to the sufferer.

1.6 What OCD is not

For partners and carers, it is particularly important to understand what OCD is not:

- It is not a reflection of true beliefs or desires.
- It is not evidence of hidden intentions or feelings.
- It is not caused by dissatisfaction or lack of love.
- It is not something that can be reasoned away.

OCD often targets the very things a person values most about their morality, responsibility, safety, identity, and relationships. Distress is not a sign of truth; it is a sign of fear.

1.7 A foundation for understanding Relationship OCD

Before exploring how OCD can centre itself around romantic relationships, it helps to recognise that relationship-focused obsessions are not a separate issue, but a specific expression of the same underlying disorder.

The brain mechanisms, learning loops, and fear responses are the same. The content may change, but the process remains consistent.

Most people experience love as a caring, supportive connection that feels nurturing and sustaining. It's a bond where giving and receiving affection come naturally, helping partners feel seen, valued, and emotionally close. Love is often experienced as a source of comfort and safety, a steady presence that can help both people carry them through life's ups and downs.

However, when someone you love is struggling with Relationship Obsessive Compulsive Disorder (ROCD), that feeling of safety can begin to feel fragile. Doubt may creep in over and over again; reassurance becomes a great need; doubts or thoughts about the relationship can turn into hours of agony; loving your partner turns out to be an emotionally taxing job that requires so much attention and care while, at the same time, trying to keep your own sanity.

You might notice feelings of confusion, grief for how the relationship once felt, or doubt about your own responses. Alongside your care and concern, you may find yourself carrying anxiety, guilt, and exhaustion without much space to acknowledge how hard this is for you too.

If you've picked up this book, you're probably feeling a mix of confusion, worry and maybe even frustration. That's normal. You are not alone. Thousands of people care for partners with ROCD, and like you, they often struggle to understand what is happening, why it's happening, and how to help without losing themselves in the process. This chapter is designed to lay the foundation and help you understand the disorder, distinguish between doubt and disorder, and begin to see your own role through the lens of clarity, compassion, and hope.

When you hear what partners' share, it is heartbreaking, as one partner shared:

"I feel broken all the time. One moment they're telling me how much they love me and in the next moment it seems like they're telling me all the reasons why they don't. I'm trying to understand that it's ROCD but it does hurt, a lot. I feel like I'm sitting inside a courtroom all day long, being tried for some crime. I do try to keep my patience intact, but some days I just feel tired, angry, lost — disappearing while trying to hold this for me and for us".

Another partner shared the exhaustion that comes with the constant uncertainty:

"I'm exhausted. I didn't know there was such a thing as ROCD, so I keep trying to tell myself it's the ROCD and not them or me but after a while, it all gets very confusing. I do give reassurance constantly, but evidently not in the right way because it doesn't work. I love him, want to help and wish there were more ways left to help. I feel I've exhausted them all and just long for the simple feeling of love before I had to start analysing it too".

Another shared a more hopeful reflection:

"It's hard watching her battle thoughts that twist everything between us. Some days I feel invisible, like I'm fighting for both of us while she's fighting her mind. We talk about moving our relationship forward, such as moving in together, and she sounds really keen. However, by the following day, or even sooner, all her doubts and uncertainty come flooding in. All I'm doing now is holding on to the good moments because that shows me our relationship is strong, so I'm sitting in hope".

Reading these stories, you can see how heavy it feels to love someone with ROCD. The confusion, the worry, the real moments of despair. It is exhausting. Beneath it all, though, is care, hope and a determination to stay connected, even when the mind of their loved one is caught in doubt.

1.8 What is Relationship Obsessive Compulsive Disorder (ROCD)

No doubt, you have probably been doing a lot of research on your own, either from your partner telling you this is what they have, or from your own surfing the web to try and make sense of your relationship.

ROCD is a form of OCD that specifically targets relationships, and quite often, romantic relationships. While OCD is widely known as manifesting as fears about germs, contamination, symmetry, or other rituals, ROCD centres on obsessive doubts and compulsions

"Carers report most commonly providing reassurance when asked to do so ... carers perceived that sufferers would feel much worse if they refused to provide reassurance".

(Kobori et al. 2017).

about love itself. Your partner might constantly question whether they really love you, whether you are "the one", or whether they are making the right choice in the relationship. Some people doubt their partner's attractiveness, compatibility, or emotional availability. These obsessions are not simply "normal relationship worries". Everyone questions their relationships from time to time, but in ROCD, the doubts are intrusive, repetitive, and anxiety-driven. They are not grounded in any objective evidence or dissatisfaction, but in the brain's compulsive need for certainty. Your partner may engage in mental rituals such as overanalysing your every word or gesture, seeking constant reassurance, comparing you to others or attempting to "test" the relationship. These actions are efforts to reduce anxiety, but they rarely succeed. Instead, they reinforce the cycle of doubt and distress.

As a carer, it can be confusing and even hurtful to witness this. And equally, ROCD sufferers do not always share their intrusive thoughts through shame, embarrassment and guilt, so you might not know the full extent of the distress in their mind. You might wonder if your partner's doubts reflect how they truly feel about you. Understanding that these compulsions stem from the disorder – and not from a lack of love – is the first step towards protecting both yourself and the relationship.

In my earlier book, "ROCD, *Is it a thing*?", I explore obsessive-compulsive disorder (OCD) and its subset, Relationship OCD (ROCD), in greater depth. You don't need to have read that book to follow this one, but if you'd like a fuller understanding of what ROCD is and how it develops, you may find it helpful to read alongside this one.

For now, this smaller overview allows us to move forward and focus on what matters most here - how to care for someone experiencing ROCD and how to look after yourself in the process. Education and understanding really do make a difference, not only to the person struggling but also to those supporting them.

Caring for someone with ROCD can be confusing and emotionally demanding. Research shows just how difficult it can be for loved ones to know what to do and *difficult it can be for loved ones to know what to do and: "Carers report most commonly providing reassurance when asked to do so ... carers perceived that sufferers would feel much worse if they refused to provide reassurance".* (Kobori et al. 2017)

1.9 How ROCD affects you

Caring for someone with ROCD can be emotionally draining. Many partners describe a constant state of vigilance by trying to anticipate triggers, managing reassurance loops and adapting their daily life in an attempt to prevent conflict or anxiety. A life that consists of walking on eggshells. This is sometimes referred to as "accommodation" or "collusion". You may find yourself performing behaviours or offering reassurances you wouldn't normally do, to help your partner feel calm, if only temporarily. A previous client of mine had literally adopted all of the OCD behaviours of their partner to try and help them.

While this comes from a place of love, it can leave you drained, anxious and resentful. It's common to experience guilt for setting boundaries, wanting a break, or feeling frustrated. It can feel as though you are "causing" their distress simply by being human, not being perfect, or having your own needs. Over time, the weight of caring for someone with ROCD can affect your own mental and physical health, your sense of identity and your sense of joy within the relationship, so whilst ROCD sucks all the joy out of the sufferer, it doesn't hold back from doing the same to you.

You are not weak or uncaring for feeling this way. ROCD is, by its nature, exhausting for both the sufferer and the partner. Recognising the emotional impact on yourself is not selfish. It is essential. The healthier you are, the better equipped you will be to support your partner.

1.10 Why your partner can't *"just snap out of it"*

It's tempting to think: if only they loved you, or if only they were more confident, they could stop the obsessing. But this is not a matter of choice or willpower. OCD is a brain-based disorder involving anxiety circuits and compulsive loops. (Stein et al., 2019). The doubts and compulsions your partner experiences are involuntary; they are usually as distressing to them as they are confusing to you.

Sometimes ROCD sufferers may appear calm one moment and anxious the next. They may reassure themselves, only to spiral again within hours. This inconsistency can be bewildering. It can feel like an emotional rollercoaster, but it's not a reflection of their commitment or love for you. Understanding this can prevent unnecessary blame and help you differentiate between the disorder and the person you care about.

Relationship OCD is not about *doubting the wrong person* — it's about a brain that misfires around uncertainty and threat. When the OCD brain detects something that feels ambiguous or important, such as love, commitment, or compatibility, it activates the same neural alarm system that alerts us to physical danger.

That alarm system is not emotional intuition. It's neurology.

Because OCD and ROCD are part of a neurobiological disorder, the intrusive doubts that show up in relationships are symptoms, not truth. They are not reflections of someone's actual values, character, or genuine level of love. They're simply the brain trying to resolve perceived threat by demanding certainty.

Understanding how the brain contributes to ROCD can help prevent unnecessary self-blame and reduce feelings of shame for both partners.

THE OCD BRAIN LOOP

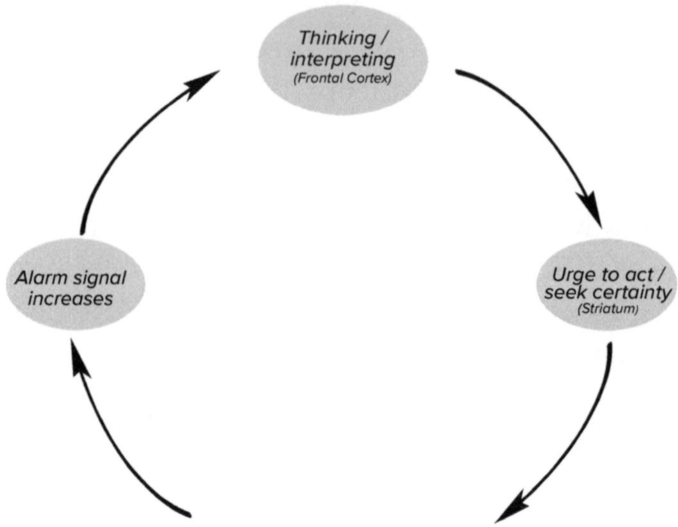

The brain is sending an alarm.
There is no fire.
(Stein et al., 2019)

1.11 Common compulsions you might see

To help you recognise ROCD dynamics, here are some familiar patterns you might notice:

1. **Reassurance Seeking:** Your partner repeatedly asks if you love them, if the relationship is "right", or if they are good enough. While initially comforting, repeated reassurance often increases dependence and anxiety.
2. **Mental Checking:** They are analysing your words, behaviours and reactions, sometimes obsessively, trying to confirm or disprove their fears.
3. **Comparison:** Your partner may compare themselves, or you, to "ideal" partners or relationships, seeking certainty that they are making the right choice.

4. **Avoidance:** Your partner might avoid situations, conversations, or people that trigger anxiety, which can feel restrictive for both of you.
5. **Emotional Withdrawal:** In moments of high doubt, your partner may seem distant, critical or "emotionally unavailable", leaving you feeling rejected or confused.

This is by no means an exhaustive list. OCD and ROCD thoughts never run out of possibilities to throw the sufferers' way.

As I mentioned earlier, it's essential to recognise that these compulsions are not a reflection of your worth or the validity of the relationship. They are manifestations of anxiety and compulsion.

1.12 Why understanding matters

The first step in helping your partner and yourself is understanding. Misunderstanding ROCD can lead to:

- You feeling responsible for your partner's anxiety.
- You engaging in accommodating behaviours that, unintentionally, reinforce compulsions.
- You losing sight of your own needs and identity.
- Putting the relationship under further emotional pressure.

By learning about ROCD, you gain perspective, tools and hope. You can approach the relationship with empathy while maintaining boundaries, communicate in ways that reduce anxiety without feeding compulsions, support your partner's journey to recovery, and keep yourself intact.

1.13 Taking care of yourself

Even in the earliest stages of understanding ROCD, I urge you to start thinking about self-care. Simple practices, such as pausing before providing reassurance, journaling your own feelings, maintaining social connections, and setting small personal boundaries, can make a significant difference. Caring for someone with ROCD is a marathon, not a sprint. Sustaining care is going to require strength, rest and compassion, for yourself as well as for your partner.

Looking ahead

In the chapters that follow, we will explore the inner workings of ROCD in more detail, delve into strategies for managing reassurance and accommodation and provide tools to create a roadmap toward recovery. You will:

- Learn how to recognise and respond to obsessive thoughts and compulsions without feeding them.
- Learn self-compassion.
- Learn how to establish personal boundaries and protect your own well-being.
- Learn practical steps for fostering connection and intimacy, even when ROCD is present.
- Learn ways to involve your partner in recovery without adding guilt or pressure.

Remember, understanding is the foundation. By learning what ROCD is and what it isn't, you are already taking the first, most important step toward creating a healthier, more compassionate relationship for both you and your loved one.

This book begins with understanding and gentle self-compassion, which is always necessary, and then gradually explores practical strategies so that you can try them in small, manageable steps. Remind yourself that you are at the very beginning of your journey, so it's okay to go slow and give yourself kindness along the way.

Taking care of someone with ROCD IS tough. There are moments when you feel patient, loving, and capable, but doubt, worry, or even tiredness can creep in. These feelings are entirely natural and don't mean you're failing. Recognising them and allowing yourself compassion are important parts of supporting both your loved one and yourself. You may question your own strength, patience, and choices. And yet, even amid this confusion, there is space for grace, resilience, and hope.

Through a compassionate lens, take a moment now. Breathe deeply, and let these words anchor you, reminding you of the care you give yourself as well as your loved one. Words you can return to as frequent, gentle reminders that your journey matters, too.

I am doing my best, and that is enough.
I can support my loved one without losing myself.
My feelings are valid, and I am allowed to express them.
It's okay to set boundaries; they protect both of us.
I am patient, compassionate, and resilient.
I do not have to fix everything; I can offer love and understanding.
I am learning and growing alongside my loved one.
Moments of doubt or frustration do not define me.
I deserve care, rest, and peace just as much as anyone else.
Each day, I take small steps toward balance and hope.

Keeping these words close builds strength for the two of you. You are doing more than you realise.

“Out of the Box” Tools for Partners

Psychological Framing: The Mirror Effect

Concept: ROCD doesn’t only affect the person who has it – it can subtly **pull you** into repetitive thoughts, doubts, or reassurance-seeking behaviours. This “mirror effect” can make you feel like you are spiralling out of control.

Practical Tips:

- Keep a journal of moments when you feel pulled into your own doubts.
- Pause and ask: “Is this my anxiety or a reaction to ROCD?”.
- Remind yourself: Doubt about my own feelings doesn’t mean the relationship is failing.

Exercise:

- Daily Mirror Check: Think about an ROCD-triggered moment. What did you actually feel, and how might ROCD have influenced your reaction?

Chapter 2

The Hidden Toll on Partners

It's natural to want to step in and help when someone you love is emotionally hurting. You want to listen, comfort, and support them. However, when you're caring for a partner with OCD or ROCD, your well-intentioned love can easily turn into something a whole lot heavier. Something that drains you rather than nourishes you. It becomes a part of your days and hours, frequently and repetitively.

Have you noticed that your energy levels are consistently low? Are you on alert, scanning for the next trigger or reassurance request? Maybe you've started to measure your days by your partner's moods: *"are they anxious today?" "Are they okay?" "What can I do to keep things calm?"*

It takes a whole lot of nervous energy, so if you're resonating with this, then this chapter is definitely for you. It's about seeing your own pain clearly and being able to name it through your experience as a carer, as a partner and noticing your feelings, and the invisible, emotional toll of living alongside ROCD. It's not about blame or guilt. It's about beginning to reclaim the space you need to breathe again. Try the *'mirror effect'* exercise at the end of the last chapter to help you practice this.

2.1 Carrying the emotional weight

It takes an act of courage to care for someone with any mental health condition. It calls for patience, empathy, and consistency in the face of unpredictability. Even the most loving person can start to feel overwhelmed when that care becomes constant and/or feels one-sided.

ROCD, with its cycles of doubt and reassurance, creates a dynamic in which you, the carer, feel like their partner and therapist. You are the steady one, the anchor, the calm voice, the comforter. Over time, this leads to emotional fatigue that can feel really debilitating.

Partners/carers often describe:

- **Exhaustion:** The mental load of managing someone else's anxiety while suppressing your own is immense.
- **Confusion:** One day, your partner feels loving and present; the next, distant or doubtful. You start questioning your own stability in the relationship.
- **Guilt:** You want to help but don't always know how. You may feel selfish for wanting time alone or resentful when your own needs go unmet.
- **Loneliness:** Even though you're in a relationship, it feels isolating when the disorder takes up so much emotional space.
- **Hyper-vigilance:** You start anticipating your partner's moods and triggers, adjusting your words and actions to keep the peace.

These experiences are not a sign that you're failing. They are signs that you've been giving deeply, perhaps too deeply, without enough replenishment.

2.2 Falling into the guilt trap

Many partners/carers fall into what I call the *"guilt trap"*. You tell yourself you should be more patient, more understanding, more supportive. You might even feel guilty for feeling frustrated, angry, or numb.

The truth is, guilt doesn't mean you don't care. It often means you care so much that you're neglecting your own emotional boundaries.

I think from time to time, it's easy to forget we are human! Human beings with limited needs and emotions of our own. Caring doesn't mean losing yourself. In fact, when you abandon your own well-being, it can harm both of you – because burnout makes empathy brittle. You can't pour from an empty cup, so we're told.

When developing these massive doses of self-compassion I mentioned earlier, ask yourself, *"If my best friend were caring for someone in my situation, what would I tell them?"*

You'd probably tell them to rest, take a break, and reach out for help. It's imperative to offer yourself that same kindness.

As you care for someone with ROCD, it's easy to pour all your energy outward and forget to offer yourself the same kindness. Self-compassion, which I explored in more detail in my previous book, can be a necessary and steady support in moments like this. As Kristin Neff reminds us, *"This is a moment of suffering. Suffering is part of life. May I be kind to myself in this moment. May I give myself the compassion I need"* (Neff, 2011).

Even a small act, such as acknowledging your own fatigue or gently reminding yourself that your efforts matter, can be powerful. Take a moment now to breathe and offer yourself a word of kindness, however small, just as you provide care to your loved one. You are learning, growing, and giving love, and you deserve a little of that care in return.

"It isn't selfish to look after yourself. It strengthens your ability to care for others".

You can nurture yourself by honouring the moments and joys that bring you happiness.

2.3 The reassurance loop: From "Do you love me?" to "Do I love you?"

Caring for someone with ROCD often means navigating a loop of reassurance. You may hear the same questions repeated, like:

- *"Do you really love me?"*
- *"Are you sure I'm the right person for you?"*
- *"You'd tell me if something was wrong, wouldn't you?"*

You'll likely respond with patience and care. You'll likely answer naturally - of course you love them! But soon, you realise the questions don't stop. The more reassurance you give, the more your partner needs it.

It's important to understand that this isn't manipulation. It's anxiety. The OCD part of their brain is screaming for certainty, and reassurance is only a short-term fix. But for you, it can feel like an emotional treadmill, where you're running hard, but you're not getting anywhere.

This pattern can wear down intimacy and spontaneity. Conversations often revolve around reassurance rather than genuine connection. You may begin to censor yourself, avoiding honesty for fear of triggering distress in your partner. Over time, that can make you feel invisible or unseen in your own relationship.

Recognising this dynamic is powerful. It means you can begin to respond with compassion and boundaries – something we'll explore in the following chapters.

As if this reassurance-seeking wasn't enough, in relationships affected by ROCD, you've probably noticed that reassurance often becomes a familiar pattern. You may be asked repeatedly, "*Do you love me*?" and respond with tenderness, comfort, and logic, **but** ROCD can just as easily flip the focus inward. The sufferer may suddenly become preoccupied with the opposite fear: *"What if I don't love you enough?"* or *"What if this relationship isn't right?"*.

This shift can be deeply confusing for you, the partner, who is doing the caring. One moment, you are being asked to provide reassurance that you love your partner; the next, you are faced with your partner's distress about whether **they** truly feel love in return. What initially appears as their fear of not being loved becomes a fear of not loving, and both fears are driven by the intrusive, doubt-fuelled cycle of ROCD, not by a lack of genuine care.

For you, the non-ROCD partner, this can create emotional whiplash. You may begin to wonder: *"Do they love me at all?"* or *"Am I enough?"*. These shifting doubts can stir insecurity and leave you feeling destabilised, unseen, or even rejected. Understanding this dynamic is essential, not because you need to take on responsibility for the ROCD, but because recognising the pattern can reduce its personalisation. These doubts are symptoms of OCD, not reflections of your worth or the true nature of your relationship.

I sincerely hope you are starting to recognise the importance of these massive doses of self-compassion you need to offer yourself. Even I am repetitive with this stipulation – for the sufferers and their partners. It is an essential requirement!

2.4 The loss that lives in the background

When you care for someone with ROCD or OCD, you might experience unspoken losses.

These can look like:

- The loss of lightness – that easy laughter and freedom couples often share.
- The loss of personal time – because your partner's needs feel urgent and constant.
- The loss of emotional reciprocity – because your worries often take a back seat.
- The loss of certainty – because the relationship feels fragile or conditional.

These losses deserve acknowledgement. You're not selfish for mourning them. Naming them helps you grieve what's changed and opens space to rebuild balance later.

2.5 "Vicarious Trauma"

Living with prolonged uncertainty, emotional strain, and vigilance can create what's sometimes called "secondary trauma" or "caregiver burnout". It's not uncommon to experience anxiety, irritability or even physical symptoms like headaches, insomnia or fatigue.

Caring for someone distressed or emotionally dysregulated can lead to secondary trauma, or *vicarious trauma* - the emotional residue of being exposed to another person's suffering (Figley, 1995).

"You don't have to fix your partner's anxiety. You can support them while allowing them to build their own resilience. Your love is part of their healing, but it is not the cure".

Over time, partners/carers may also experience caregiver burnout, a state of emotional, physical, and mental exhaustion that arises when the demands of caregiving outweigh the resources available to cope (Maslach & Leiter, 2016). Burnout doesn't happen because you are weak - it emerges when you have been strong for too long without receiving support or rest.

You might also develop a "rescuer" identity by feeling responsible for your partner's stability. It can become hard to relax and trust that things won't fall apart without your constant watchfulness.

Here's something to hold on to:

2.6 Permission to step back

Healthy caring involves balance. You can be compassionate without being consumed by it. You can be supportive without being responsible for every outcome.

What do these "permissions" look like?

Start by permitting yourself to:

- Take breaks from emotional conversations when you need rest.
- Say *"I love you, but I can't reassure you right now – maybe we can talk about this later"*.
- Pursue hobbies, friendships and time alone without guilt.
- Reach out for your own therapy or support.

Stepping back doesn't mean stepping away. It's an act of self-respect. It means creating healthy boundaries and offering yourself generous and healthy doses of self-compassion as you learn to hold them, because this isn't a one-time task. You may notice that I have already mentioned "generous and healthy doses" of self-compassion more than once, and I will continue to do so - not by accident, but because it is vital and you will need this reminder. You will return to this compassion repeatedly, much as you will to the personal boundaries you introduce, possibly needing to reinforce them on more than one occasion.

"Even in stormy seas, you can be a steady ship. Boundaries are your anchor, self-compassion your ballast. You can care deeply, protect yourself, and navigate the waves with calm and presence".

A Steady Ship

2.7 Nurturing your own anxiety

When you've spent so long focusing on someone else's distress, reconnecting with your own self might feel foreign. You may have forgotten what relaxes you or what brings you joy.

Start small to reconnect with yourself.

- Take a quiet walk without your phone.
- Spend an hour doing something creative or nourishing.
- Write down three things that went well today.
- Notice when your body feels calm and what helps it feel that way.

Your sense of self is not a luxury; it is a necessity. The stronger and more grounded you are, the more loving and stable you can be in your relationship.

ROCD creates tension, doubt and emotional fatigue in you, the partner.

You may remember in the *"How to Use this Book"* section that I promised some creative ideas to help you navigate some of the complexities of ROCD. Whilst strategies will be introduced and explained in all the chapters, with traditional advice focusing on boundaries and reassurance, at the end of some chapters, there will be some "out of the box" tools you might not have thought of. These ideas introduce creative, practical and slightly unconventional strategies to help you stay grounded, compassionate and resilient.

"Out of the box" Tool for Partners

Emotional Budgeting

Concept: Think of your emotional energy like a budget. ROCD interactions can drain it quickly, so partners can plan how much "emotional currency" to spend on reassurance, discussions, or tension-filled moments.

Practical Tips:

- Allocate a daily or weekly "emotional allowance" for ROCD interactions.

- Once the allowance is spent, take a restorative break, like a walk, a coffee or time with friends.
- This helps you avoid burnout and maintain perspective.

Exercise Idea:

- Make a small chart, listing the typical ROCD triggers you face, assign an "emotional cost" (1-5), and track your spending. Notice patterns where you need to add more self-care.

Moving forward

This chapter has been about seeing yourself clearly, not just as a partner, but as a person with your own needs and limits. You've probably given a lot, and it's ok to admit you're tired.

In the next chapter, to deepen empathy, we'll take some time to understand what's going on in the mind of a ROCD sufferer and then move on to explore how to set boundaries that protect both you and your partner. In an ROCD relationship, boundaries are not barriers; they are essential. They serve as anchors, allowing each person to care without becoming overwhelmed. Neither do boundaries distance you from one another. They create the conditions where love can feel safe rather than strained by anxiety or fear.

Chapter 3

Deeper Understanding of the ROCD Mind

I've written this chapter not to make excuses for an ROCD sufferer's behaviour, but to help you build understanding of what goes through your partner's inner world, in a way that deepens empathy and helps prepare you for boundary setting, which we'll look at in the following chapter.

Loving someone with ROCD can feel very unsettling. One day everything feels calm and loving, and the next, you're caught up in a torrent of questions and doubts, and the discomfort of them pulling away and creating emotional distance, which becomes very confusing, leaving you wondering why they can't believe you or see that everything is ok.

Let's step inside their experience for a moment, not to get lost in it, but to see the landscape they are navigating. Behind the behaviours you see - the reassurance seeking, the checking, the sudden coldness - there's usually something a lot deeper, like fear. The more you can build understanding around ROCD, the more you will recognise how important it is to take care of yourself while caring for them.

What's common to all forms of OCD is that it's built on the same structure - an intrusive (repetitive/obsessive) thought or fear which triggers anxiety. The person carries out a ritual or mental activity in an attempt to relieve their anxiety. That relief is usually temporary, so the cycle repeats. Over time, these behaviours become automatic - the brain's misguided attempt to protect itself from uncertainty.

In ROCD, many intrusive thoughts latch onto love, for example, attraction, intelligence, compatibility or morality in relationships. Thoughts I hear from clients often sound like:

- *"What if I don't really love my partner?"*
- *"What if I'm only in the relationship because I'm scared to be alone?"*
- *"What if they're not 'the one'?"*
- *"What if I'm leading them on or lying by staying in the relationship?"*

They can also sound like statements, "I don't love my partner, etc, which also generate anxiety and emotional distress. I'm mentioning these "statement-type" thoughts because many ROCD clients feel that a "statement" may hold more certainty than a question.

For non-ROCD sufferers, these might seem like passing worries that fade after a good conversation or moment of connection. For someone with ROCD, these thoughts bring a lot of fear and intense anxiety. They come with a sense of urgency or immediacy to solve the question and seek certainty.

3.1 Searching for certainty

OCD/ROCD is frequently called the 'doubting disorder'. The brain demands 100% proof that the relationship is right and emotionally perfect. The sufferer will spend hours analysing every feeling, conversation, tone of voice, and facial expression for hidden meaning.

You might see your partner mentally scanning for evidence that confirms or disproves their fears:

- *"Did my heart race when they kissed me? If not, maybe I don't love them enough".*

- *"They just annoyed me then – does that mean we are incompatible?".*
- *"I felt attracted to someone else. Does that mean I'm with the wrong person? Does it mean I have emotionally cheated?".*

Every emotion, every reaction becomes data to dissect, but because emotions ebb and flow naturally, the 'evidence' keeps changing, therefore feeding the cycle of doubt.

Relentless monitoring of emotions and reactions is exhausting and overwhelming.

This is the daily reality for people with ROCD - constantly questioning their feelings and never being able to trust their own heart.

3.2 Attachment styles: for a contextual lens (not a strategy)

I've included this section to help *you make sense of what you are witnessing*, and not to give you something to analyse, fix or apply to your partner.

However, I strongly recommend that you don't skip the following paragraphs, which explain what this section is NOT for, before I give a brief overview of attachment styles.

What this section is not for

To protect both you and your partner, it's essential to be clear about the limits of attachment theory in the context of ROCD. It is **not** intended to help you diagnose or label your partner's attachment style, encourage monitoring or interpreting their behaviour through a psychological lens, give you another way to manage, reassure or stabilise their anxiety or suggest that better understanding will resolve ROCD.

"Insight is helpful only when it brings you back to yourself"

Trying to work out *which* attachment style your partner has can become part of the reassurance loop, especially when OCD is present. It might feel like being insightful or caring, but it often increases hypervigilance, emotional exhaustion and the taking on of responsibility that does not belong to you.

I am offering you an overview of what attachment theory is about to help you notice what gets **activated in you** when uncertainty, rejection or emotional distance arises; to help you understand why ROCD can feel so personally destabilising, even when you know it is a condition; and also help you stay grounded in your own boundaries, needs and reality.

You are **not** your partner's therapist, regulator, or cure. Understanding ROCD and the stress it can place on attachment systems is about self-protection and clarity, not intervention. If, at any point, you notice yourself analysing, tracking or trying to work out what your partner's behaviour "means", gently return to this principle:

Anything that pulls you further into managing someone else's anxiety is not insight - it's erosion.

3.3 Attachment theory

Attachment theory, first introduced by John Bowlby, provides a framework for understanding how early experiences with caregivers shape the ways people form emotional bonds and seek security throughout life (Bowlby, 1969). Bowlby observed that children are biologically wired to seek closeness and safety from their caregivers, and that the quality of these early relationships has a lasting impact on emotional regulation, trust, and intimacy in adulthood. Secure early attachments generally help children feel confident as they explore the world, knowing they can rely on a responsive caregiver. In contrast, inconsistent or unavailable caregiving can lead to anxious or avoidant patterns, shaping how people later in life manage closeness, uncertainty, and reassurance. Mary Ainsworth's research, including her well-known "Strange Situation" study, identified three attachment patterns — secure, anxious, and avoidant — by observing how children responded to separations and reunions with their caregivers (Ainsworth et al., 1978). These patterns often continue into adult relationships, influencing how people experience closeness, handle conflict, and respond to uncertainty or reassurance. They can help explain why certain behaviours or worries appear in romantic and close relationships.

For partners supporting someone with ROCD, attachment theory is not a tool for analysing, judging, or trying to "fix" your loved one. Instead, it offers a way to understand why specific thoughts, doubts, or behaviours may arise, and why they can feel persistent or intense. Recognising these patterns can enhance awareness, empathy, and patience, helping you respond compassionately without taking responsibility for controlling or managing the ROCD. Understanding attachment allows you to see the relational context and the emotional needs behind behaviours - both your partner's and your own - and to approach the relationship with insight, kindness, and understanding rather than correction.

It's important to note that some of the thoughts or worries experienced in ROCD may be influenced by attachment patterns, but this is not always the case. While attachment theory can provide helpful insight into why specific fears or doubts feel especially strong, many ROCD-related thoughts arise primarily from the disorder itself, rather than from a person's attachment style. In other words, sometimes there is a connection, and sometimes there isn't — the key is to recognise that ROCD behaviours are fear-driven, not a definitive reflection of someone's relational patterns.

That being said, understanding attachment can help you:

- Stop personalising sudden withdrawal, doubt or emotional volatility.

- Reduce self-blame and the urge to “be better” to stabilise the relationship.
- Recognise why reassurance, closeness or logic may temporarily soothe, but ultimately fuel, anxiety.

I want to reaffirm that this understanding is offered as context, not an explanation. It might help you answer the question *“Why does this feel so destabilising for me?”* rather than *“What is wrong with my partner?*.

Many of my clients or their partners often mention their attachment styles, sometimes based on research they’ve done themselves or from online quizzes or questionnaires they’ve tried on social media. While these insights can be interesting, it’s important to remember that self-identified attachment labels may not always reflect a person’s stable relational patterns, especially in the context of ROCD, where fear-driven thoughts and behaviours can temporarily influence how someone responds in a relationship.

3.4 How it feels on the inside for the ROCD Sufferer

This is a usual inner monologue that my clients share with me when in the grips of an ROCD spiral.

- *“I love them, but what if it’s not real love?”*
- *“What if I’m fooling myself?”*
- *“What if they deserve better?”*
- *“What if I’m just ‘settling’?”*
- *“What if I’m just comfortable?”*
- *“What if I realise I made a mistake in a few years?”*

It’s important to note that these “what if” questions and/or statements can revert to doubts about the partner’s love as well as their own. As I explained earlier, OCD is not picky and never runs out of possibilities to throw your partner’s way.

When I say ‘in the grips of an ROCD spiral’ - imagine those thoughts repeating themselves dozens of times a day. No matter how many reassurances they get or the temporary relief from anxiety, reassurance doesn’t calm the root fear - *‘uncertainty’*. You might also see an ‘ROCD spiral’ described as an OCD loop or vicious cycle.

Most ROCD sufferers describe feeling:

- Terrified - that they will hurt their partner by staying in the relationship if their doubts are ‘true’.
- Guilt and Embarrassment - for having the doubts in the first place.
- Ashamed - because they know their fears don’t make logical sense.
- Desperate - for certainty, to know, once and for all, that they’ve made the ‘right’ choice.

It’s an endless cycle of love and fear.

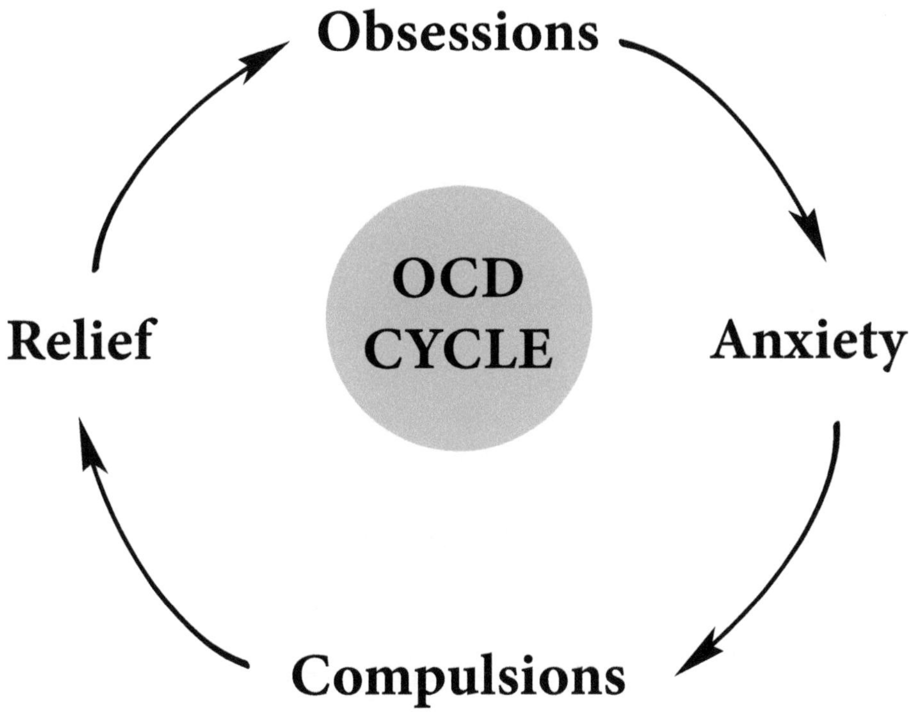

3.5 How it feels on the inside for YOU

As a partner, you might experience what feels like emotional whiplash. One day, your partner is affectionate and connected, and the next, they're distant, critical, or withdrawn. You might take that shift personally - who wouldn't?

It can be challenging to get your head around the fact that these changes have little or nothing to do with you. It's about how much anxiety your partner is experiencing inside. When the obsessive thoughts flare up, they can't trust their feelings. Their brain is telling them something is 'off', so they withdraw or test you to check if it's true.

It's a painful watch - and painful to experience.

It helps to remember that this behaviour isn't a reflection of your worth or their genuine love for you. It's an anxiety symptom and not a measure of love.

3.6 Common triggers and compulsions

While every person's ROCD looks a little different, here are some common patterns that you probably notice:

- **Reassurance seeking** - asking you to confirm your love or compatibility repeatedly.
- **Testing behaviours** - picking fights or analysing your responses to see if you'll 'react' correctly.
- **Rumination** - mentally replaying moments in the relationship, searching for signs that something is wrong.
- **Avoidance** - pulling away emotionally or physically to see how they feel about the distance.
- **Comparison** - measuring your relationship against others to see if it 'stacks up'.

Each of these behaviours is a way of coping with uncertainty - but ironically, it only serves to make the uncertainty and their anxiety stronger.

3.7 It's not about you (even when it feels like it is)

One of the hardest things for partners to accept is that their partner's doubts aren't really about them. They're about the sufferer's relationship with uncertainty, perfectionism and fear.

When your partner says, *"I don't know if I love you"*, it's likely going to sound and feel like a rejection. Internally, it's more them reaching out for reassurance: *"I don't feel safe in my own feelings right now. Help me feel sure"*.

Understanding this doesn't ease the hurt, but it can shift your perspective. It allows you to respond with steadiness instead of defensiveness.

3.8 Why reassurance doesn't work

It's completely natural to want to reassure your partner. You love them, you want to calm them. Unfortunately, each time you provide reassurance, the brain's anxiety circuit learns - *"I can't handle doubt without checking"*. That means, the next time uncertainty arises - and it always does - the brain demands even more reassurance.

I work with supporting partners to *step out of the reassurance loop*. It doesn't mean you are withholding love. It means learning to show care in ways that support long-term healing rather than temporary relief. I'll show you how to do this in more detail in Chapter 4.

3.9 Can the brain re-learn?

Yes, OCD/ROCD is a treatable condition. With the right therapy (especially cognitive behaviour therapy and exposure response prevention), self-awareness, and support, people can learn to tolerate uncertainty and stop feeding the obsession-compulsion cycle.

Here is what OCDAction says about OCD.

"OCD is a severe disorder. But it is treatable"

"OCD is a clinically recognised disorder which affects around 1-2% of the population. It is debilitating and paralysing. People with OCD experience intensely negative, repetitive and intrusive thoughts, combined with a chronic feeling of doubt or danger (obsessions). To quell the thought or quieten the anxiety, they will often repeat an action, again and again (compulsions)."

"One of the greatest challenges that people with OCD face is the need to fight both the all pervasive stigma of mental health disorders and the widely held belief that OCD is a mild or even "quirky" problem that is nothing more than hand washing. People might use the phrase "a bit OCD" without understanding the onerous nature of this severe condition and its impact." (https://ocdaction.org.uk/learn-about-ocd/

You can support your loved one in accessing available treatments for OCD through reputable providers, such as OCDAction and explore further what cognitive behaviour therapy and exposure response prevention look like, including recommended medications like SSRIs (Selective Serotonin Reuptake Inhibitors).

Recovery doesn't mean having no doubts. It means learning to live with them peacefully - to see a thought like, *"What if I don't really love my partner?"* and think, *"That's my OCD talking, I don't have to engage with it."* It is usual for wayward intrusive thoughts to pop into our minds from time to time, and for the non-OCD sufferer, they can brush them off. When these thoughts become obsessive and repetitive, causing deep distress, then this style of thinking is considered extreme, and OCD might be possible. I think it's also appropriate here to include what I had mentioned in my earlier book, "ROCD, *Is it a thing?"* – that working with ROCD is not about repairing an already deteriorating relationship that holds no value, but working with irrational thoughts that are entirely at odds with the reality of the relationship.

3.10 What can you do – RIGHT NOW!

Here are a few small, but powerful, things you can start practising today:

- **Name the disorder, not the person** - when you feel hurt or confused, remind yourself "This is the ROCD speaking". It helps separate your partner's identity from their symptoms.
- **Pause reassuring** - if your partner asks for reassurance, try a gentle re-direct, *"I sense you're feeling anxious right now. How can we sit with that feeling instead of trying to solve it?"*
- **Encourage therapy** - Exposure and response prevention (ERP) is the most effective treatment. Support your partner's recovery, but remember it's their journey. I have included some additional resources at the back of the book if your partner is open to therapy.

- **Keep perspective** - there will be good days and difficult ones. Progress isn't linear, but every step towards awareness counts.

I think it's an important "first" towards recovery for the ROCD sufferer and the carer to be able to access a strategy early on towards building self-awareness, because thoughts are so automatic, and it's really easy to get tangled up in them and apply meaning. I implement a strategy almost immediately for my ROCD clients by introducing what's called 'non-engagement responses'. This helps the sufferer build self-awareness through curiosity, by naming the thought as an 'anxious thought' or 'ROCD thought' and working towards separating their identity from their symptoms - as I shared above, naming the disorder, not the person. This doesn't mean 'automatic recovery' - it's one of the strategies towards building resilience and tolerating the anxiety using a brand new toolbox.

Out of the Box Tools for Partners

Concept:

Using metaphors to externalise ROCD helps you avoid personalising obsessive thoughts and reduces frustration.

Examples:

- Imagine thoughts as "clouds passing through your mind, rather than a judgment of the relationship.
- Imagine the ROCD as a cartoon or character – something silly, not threatening.

- Name the intrusive thought like a recurring TV character: *"Here comes Captain Doubt again."*

Exercise Idea:

- Keep a small notebook of metaphors for ROCD moments. Whenever doubt arises, refer to it to shift perspective and lighten tension.

With my ROCD clients, I use metaphors a lot. Using a metaphor allows you to see an experience *from the outside*, rather than feeling consumed by it. When something is described through a metaphor, it helps create a little distance - enough space to observe the pattern, understand it more clearly, and reduce the emotional weight of "owning" it.

Metaphors act like a lens: they simplify what's tangled, soften what feels overwhelming, and help you view the situation with curiosity (another of my favourite words when exploring ROCD with sufferers) instead of self-blame. This distance often makes it easier to work with complex thoughts or emotions, rather than feeling defined or controlled by them.

Looking ahead

Now that you have a clearer picture of what's happening inside the ROCD mind and some starting strategies, the next step is learning how to respond in ways that protect you and empower them.

In the next chapter, I'll explain boundaries that can help heal both of you - how to love without enabling and how to create a relationship where care flows in both directions.

“I am learning, and that is enough”

Chapter 4

Boundaries that heal both of you

While caring for someone with ROCD, you've probably found yourself walking on eggshells.

You want to help your partner, you want to comfort them, but no matter what you say, the doubt seems to creep back. You reassure and relax......... for a moment. Then a new question, a new "what if?" appears, and you're right back where you started.

There's a fine and invisible line between *helping and feeding* the ROCD cycle, which is one of the most complex parts of loving someone with OCD or ROCD.

Love without boundaries can quickly turn into exhaustion. For your partner, and for yourself, setting boundaries with compassion can become one of the most healing forces in your relationship.

4.1 The struggle with boundaries

The instinct to soothe someone you love when they are suffering runs deep. You might think:

- *"They'll calm down if I give them reassurance".*
- *"They'll think I don't care if I don't answer their question".*
- *They need me more than I need to rest, so I can handle this".*

Over time, this constant emotional firefighting takes its toll on you. Your own anxiety creeps in, and you feel drained and sometimes resentful. Rather than connecting as two people, the relationship starts revolving around managing the ROCD.

Setting boundaries can be difficult and feel cruel, almost leaving you feeling like you are withholding love. Truthfully, though, setting boundaries is a deeper form of love. Boundaries say, *"I believe you are capable of facing this", "I love you enough not to feed the very thing that hurts you"*.

4.2 Accommodation

There's actually a name for the ways partners/carers get pulled into OCD cycles – it's called **accommodation**.

It means doing things to relieve your partner's anxiety - checking, answering questions, avoiding triggers, or participating in compulsions/rituals. It's always done out of love, but it accidentally strengthens the disorder's grip.

*The term accommodation has been used to refer to family responses related explicitly to obsessive-compulsive (OC) symptoms: it encompasses behaviors such as directly participating in compulsions, assisting a relative with obsessive-compulsive disorder (OCD) when he/she is performing a ritual, or helping him/her to avoid triggers that may precipitate obsessions and compulsions (*https://pubmed.ncbi.nlm.nih.gov/*)*

"Accommodation" in ROCD might look like:

- Reassuring your partner repeatedly that you love them or that your relationship is "right".
- Avoiding people, movies or situations that trigger their doubts.
- Revisiting or going over arguments endlessly or over-explaining your feelings.
- Whenever your partner's anxiety spikes, you agree to "take a break" or "test the relationship" in some way that your partner requests.

These actions can feel compassionate in the moment as they can ease distress. Unfortunately, in the long term, they reinforce the message: *"You can't handle uncertainty without me helping you"*.

The goal is to care in ways that foster growth rather than dependency.

4.3 Build a bridge, not a wall.

Boundaries do not shut your partner out; they define an environment that makes both of you feel safe, supported, and understood. They say: *"This is what I can offer." "This is what I can't do for you." "We can face this together."*

Think of a bridge between two people. Without it, the gap can seem significant and fears, suspicions or misreadings have plenty of room to grow. With the bridge, sharing and support can flow in both ways; this helps you keep close and carry the link on your walk through an unsure path.

When your partner seeks reassurance:

"I don't want to feed the OCD by answering that. I know this feels scary, but how about we sit with the discomfort together?"

When your partner wants you to avoid triggers:

"Let me support you while you face the anxiety, as avoiding it only keeps the fear alive".

When YOU need emotional space:

"I love you, but I'm feeling drained right now. I'm going to take some time to recharge so I can show up for you properly later".

When YOU want to shift focus:

"Let's talk about something other than the doubts for a while. Tell me about your day, not your OCD".

This way, you are validating your partner's feelings and gently reminding them that healing means facing, not escaping, uncertainty.

Good communication turns boundaries from ***silent expectations*** *into* ***shared understanding.***

4.4 The emotional guilt trap

Partners often struggle with guilt, thinking that if they don't help, they'll think they don't care, or that if they say no, they'll spiral, or that it's easier to give in than to see them suffer.

It's understandable to feel this way, yet every time you give in to it, you teach the OCD that it can control both of you through fear.

By reframing guilt as a sign that you're doing something new, not something wrong, you can also learn to sit with the discomfort, which is not the same as harm. It's precisely how recovery begins.

4.5 Setting boundaries without conflict

Communication is key when you begin setting boundaries because it turns your internal needs into something your partner can actually understand and respond to. Boundaries only work when they are expressed clearly, calmly and consistently. Otherwise, your partner may guess, assume, or misinterpret your intentions.

Open communication reduces conflict, builds trust, and helps both sides feel respected. It also gives you a chance to state your needs without guilt, and allows your partner to adjust, collaborate, or clarify.

Here are some ideas to help you:

- **Lead with empathy, not authority:** Instead of *"You need to stop asking me that", try "I can see this is really distressing and I want to help you face it differently".*
- **Use "I" statements:** Using "I" statements leads to better communication and understanding and helps reduce defensiveness and conflict. You could say, *"I feel overwhelmed when I'm asked to give reassurance all the time,"* rather than *"You're making me anxious".*

- **Be consistent:** Consistency builds trust. If you sometimes give reassurance and sometimes don't, then your partner's brain learns to keep trying "just in case".
- **Expect pushback:** As for many people on the receiving end of a new boundary being set, your partner's anxiety may spike. This is normal when you first change your responses, as OCD will likely test the old pattern. Try to remain calm, kind and steady.
- **Celebrate small wins:** Hope grows in every moment that your partner tolerates uncertainty, if only for a few seconds. Notice it, praise it. Every step forward is progress.

4.6 Protect your own energy.

It is emotionally intense caring for someone with ROCD. Your well-being is one of the most essential stabilising forces in the relationship, even if you do feel that your needs come second.

When you take care of yourself, you're showing up for what a healthy balance looks like. Your partner needs to learn this, too.

Here are some small, but powerful practices you can try:

- **Take intentional breaks:** it is ok to take a step back, even for an hour, to reset.
- **Connect with friends and family:** you need your own support network.
- **Seek professional help if you need it:** many therapists offer sessions for carers to help navigate setting boundaries, and if they are knowledgeable about OCD and it's complexities, then even better, which is what I would recommend.
- **Do things that bring you joy:** You are a whole person in your own right, not just a supporter for your loved one.

If your boundary feels 'wishy washy'

You're likely to have days when you slip into reassurance-giving or say yes when you meant no. That's normal. Boundaries aren't rigid walls and can take time to grow. Plus, unexpected situations or changes happen all the time. If your boundaries are too strict and inflexible, it can make it hard to adapt. A little flexibility allows you to respond appropriately without feeling guilty or compromised.

Relationships do require some give-and-take, so a little flexibility can help you maintain connection and empathy without sacrificing your own needs or adding unnecessary stress. Boundaries need to be realistic, as life involves compromise, nuance, and context. Absolute rules can be isolating or impractical, while flexible boundaries are sustainable and human.

If you do find yourself back in the reassurance loop, try to reflect gently and compassionately, because it's likely you slipped into old habits because you love them, and you don't have to be perfect to make a difference - just aware.

I think that there's an important distinction to make here, between what **your healthy boundaries** can look like versus what your partner's **ROCD boundaries** might be perceived as, when spoken through an OCD lens and OCD's quest for certainty.

Boundaries are essential for healthy relationships - they protect our well-being, clarify what's acceptable and help us feel safe. They work best when they have a little flexibility, allowing us to adapt to life's unpredictable moments. For someone with ROCD, what might look like a boundary can actually be a form of control. Instead of protecting well-being, these "boundaries" are often rigid rules meant to manage anxiety, monitor thoughts, or control a partner's behaviour. Healthy boundaries create calm and connection. ROCD boundaries tend to fuel obsession, guilt and fear. The difference comes down to intention and flexibility - real boundaries protect and support, while control-driven boundaries trap the mind.

"Healthy boundaries"
Boundaries can keep us safe, but this rigid circle shows fear at work – trapping the ROCD sufferer and keeping you on the outside.

4.7 The gift of loving detachment

"Loving detachment" is a phrase that sounds a bit cold, but is actually deeply compassionate. It means staying emotionally available while refusing to be pulled into anxiety's drama. It's one of the greatest gifts you can offer yourself and the person you care about.

It's not about distance or coldness, but a decision to stay rooted in your own centre, while allowing the other person the dignity of their own journey. When you detach with love, you soften your grip on outcomes and loosen the fear that tells us we must fix, rescue or carry what was never ours. You learn to stand alongside your partner, to be supportive without absorbing, and to remain compassionate without losing yourself.

This is where loving detachment meets boundaries.

Boundaries mark where you end, and another person begins.

Loving detachment is the way you hold those boundaries with kindness rather than guilt or defensiveness.

Detachment gives boundaries breathing space, reassuring you that saying what you can or can't offer doesn't make you unloving; it makes you authentic.

Boundaries and loving detachment create clearer, calmer and more honest relationships. You will find that your connection can grow when you are both allowed to be whole, and love doesn't have to be earned through sacrifice.

Example of loving detachment in practice

Sam has ROCD. He constantly seeks reassurance about his relationship with Alex, particularly when times are tough. Wanting to be loving and supportive, Alex used to respond quickly, repeating reassurances to help Sam feel better. At first, it seemed helpful for quite some time until she began to feel worn down while quietly taking on the responsibility of keeping Sam calm.

When Alex began practising loving detachment, it was awkward. The first time Alex decided not to reassure, guilt immediately set in: Am I being mean? Am I leaving them in their hour of need? Rather than pulling away, Alex stayed with her feelings and responded softly: "I can see how anxious you are, and I care about you. I'm not going to answer this question right now, but I'm here with you while this feeling passes."

Though it was hard to sit with Sam's pain, Alex slowly saw a shift, not only in Sam but also in herself. There was ease in no longer having to carry the weight to chase away the worry. Loving detachment didn't mean loving less; it meant caring in a way that didn't add fuel to the fear. With time, the tie felt softer, sharper, and more durable.

Why loving detachment helps

Research shows that while reassurance can soothe anxiety briefly, it often strengthens fear over time by teaching the brain that reassurance is needed to feel safe (Abramowitz et al., 2012).

When you stay present without answering fear-driven questions, your loved one has the opportunity to learn, slowly and imperfectly, that anxiety can rise and fall on its own. This supports resilience and self-trust, while also protecting you from becoming emotionally overextended or caught in repeated reassurance cycles (Salkovskis et al., 1999).

4.8 If you're scared you're causing harm

Most individuals fear that reducing reassurance might appear aloof, unkind, or even harmful. Such fears typically stem from love rather than neglect. Practising loving detachment does not involve disregarding pain or withdrawing affection; it involves providing steadiness rather than certainty. Changing long-standing patterns can make you feel guilty or doubtful; this should not be taken as an indication that you're doing something wrong. It is often a sign that you are moving toward responses that foster long-term emotional health for the two of you.

In the next chapter, we'll move from boundaries to navigating recovery. It's not an exercise in fixing what is broken but one of walking gently with yourself to find clarity and learn to trust your own mind again.

Chapter 5

A Pathway Out of the Fog

A pathway out of the fog means you're looking to move through uncertainty with patience, compassion and confidence in your own mind. This chapter includes steps to help you gain more clarity and trust in yourself.

Along the way, you will continue to put into practice the gift of loving detachment and the ability to hold your own boundaries with kindness, as I shared in Chapter 4, to help you support your partner without absorbing their struggles; and to care deeply without losing yourself.

In time, your path will become clearer, not because the fog disappears overnight but because you are learning to walk with steadiness and care. The path isn't going to look like a straight line because that's not the journey of living with ROCD. Sometimes it might feel like one step forward, one back, sometimes sideways and sometimes just standing still and catching your breath.

Some days the fog lifts, and clarity feels close at hand; you feel that closeness you both want and feel settled, and then other days the fog thickens and old doubts resurface. Every step matters, however small, because it builds resilience, self-trust, and strength that eventually carry you through.

Your instinct might be to fix things, to make your partner feel better, to calm their fears, to find the "right" words. That's completely natural, but recovery begins when you shift from ***fixer*** to ***supporter***.

5.1 Shifting from "Fixer" to "Supporter"

Supporting your partner means walking alongside them as they learn to sit with their discomfort, rather than trying to rescue them.

This shift reduces pressure, restores balance and empowers your partner to develop their own coping tools – something reassurance can never do.

- **Stepping back from solving**

  Resist the urge to reassure or provide answers – focus on being present and calm. Your support is about stability and not solutions. So, instead of thinking *"How can I make this anxiety go away?"* try *"How can I help them face this anxiety safely?"*.

- **Practice "loving detachment"**

  Listening validates their experience without reinforcing compulsions and also enables you to acknowledge their feelings without taking responsibility for fixing their uncertainty. So, if they say *"I'm not sure I really love you"*, try reflecting *"It sounds like you're feeling really unsure right now"*.

- **Encourage self-management**

  Support your partner in using their coping strategies, therapy exercises, or journaling. Phrases like *"I trust you to use the tools you've been learning"* empower them to take ownership of their recovery.

- **Manage your own anxiety**

  Recognise if your partner's anxiety triggers your own anxiety, leading to an urge to intervene. Take a breath, pause, and remind yourself that staying calm and consistent is far more helpful than "fixing".

- **Stay consistent and predictable**

  Being a steady presence to your partner is far more reassuring than repeated arguments or explanations ever will be. Consistency builds trust without reinforcing OCD cycles.

- **Model self-compassion**

  Show that it's ok to have limits, feel frustrated or need space. By taking care of yourself, you demonstrate balanced support and healthy boundaries.

- **Setting boundaries around conversations**

  For example, a gentle boundary might be you saying, *"I care about you and want to support you, but I can't answer that question every time it comes up"*, or *"Let's try a strategy from your therapist instead"*.

- **Celebrating small wins together**

  When moments occur when your partner manages their anxiety without compulsions, praise their effort and resilience, not certainty. This reinforces recovery behaviours without feeding the OCD cycle.

- **Remembering the bigger picture**

  Recovery is not linear. Some days may well feel like steps backwards, and it's very common. Stay supportive, calm and loving. Your role is to walk beside them, not carry them.

It makes sense here to pause and maybe review Chapter 2, where I discuss healthy caring that involves balance and the importance of reconnecting with yourself. Sometimes, going back to a chapter can gently remind you how the ideas fit together and support one another.

5.2 Understanding evidence-based therapies

You are not looking to become your partner's therapist, but knowing a little about what works for OCD can help you support them. As we've explored, recovery from ROCD is not about "fixing" your partner or making their doubts go away; it's about helping them learn to respond differently to the intrusive thoughts that drive anxiety.

As a partner/carer, you can encourage your partner to work with a therapist trained in OCD treatment, learn about ERP together so you understand what they're trying to do, and celebrate their exposures – those brave moments when they choose to face doubt rather than escape it.

Healing comes through *doing*, not avoiding. Your calm presence can help make those steps less frightening.

Here's a brief overview of these therapies, including their goals, techniques, and benefits, all of which I use in my one-to-one therapy sessions with ROCD clients as a roadmap to recovery. If you're reading "ROCD, *Is it a thing"* alongside this book, then you will find all of the techniques explained thoroughly and how to do them, and I believe you will also find them an excellent resource for yourself.

I highly recommend a compassionate, values-led approach as it's not only the ROCD sufferer who can experience low self-esteem and self-worth – your own can take a bit of a battering also!

Much of what I share in this book and "ROCD, *Is it a thing?"* comes from years of working as a therapist and from listening closely to the experiences of people living with ROCD. My aim has always been to offer practical, lived insight rather than theory alone. That said, when we explore specific therapeutic approaches - such as CBT with ERP, Acceptance and Commitment Therapy (ACT), or mindfulness-based strategies - I also cite scientific research.

These citations aren't meant to replace experience or empathy, but to show that the methods discussed have been tested and supported in studies. They offer reassurance that the tools and strategies you read about have a solid evidence base, while still honouring the human side of recovery. There are references and a bibliography at the back of this book if you are interested in further reading, but for now, here is a brief overview of the approaches and their goals.

Cognitive Behaviour Therapy (CBT) with Exposure Response Prevention (ERP) are two of the most widely studied and practical approaches for OCD, and its various themes.

The Goal is to reduce compulsions, challenge unhelpful thought patterns and lean into anxiety. Your role as partner/carer is to support without rescuing, encourage ERP practice and maintain a calm presence.

Mindfulness-based approaches

The Goal is to develop awareness of thoughts and feelings without judgment, noticing them as temporary experiences rather than truths that must be acted on.

Techniques to use are mindful breathing, body scans and observing intrusive thoughts without reacting.

The benefits of this approach include reducing rumination and anxiety and helping tolerate uncertainty.

Acceptance & Commitment Therapy (ACT/Values-led approaches)

The Goal is to increase psychological flexibility, helping your partner live according to their values rather than OCD rules.

Techniques involve accepting uncomfortable thoughts and feelings rather than fighting them. Clarifying personal values (e.g. love, honesty and kindness) and taking committed actions in line with them.

The benefits help your partner move forward in life, even while uncertainty or intrusive thoughts remain.

Compassion-focused approaches

The Goal is to reduce self-criticism and shame, which are common in ROCD.

Techniques include self-compassion exercises, guided imagery and compassionate self-talk.

Benefits create a gentler internal environment, reducing the urge to check, reassure or control.

Psychoeducation and structured support

Learning about OCD and ROCD helps both you and your partner understand the nature of intrusive thoughts and compulsions and the recovery process. You, the partner, know how to respond without reassurance-giving, encourage ERP, and maintain boundaries.

Lifestyle and well-being strategies (complementary support)

Encourages stress management by exploring sleep hygiene, gentle exercise and relaxation techniques. Keeping track of triggers and progress by journaling can be helpful, as can social support that encourages connection without over-reliance on reassurance.

5.3 Build an environment that supports recovery

Your home and daily life can either fuel OCD or gently starve it.

You don't have to change everything overnight, but you can create an environment where recovery feels possible.

Here are a few ideas:

- **Keep routines stable:** Consistency calms the nervous system.
- **Make space for rest and joy:** OCD thrives in stress; joy is its quiet antidote.
- **Use shared language:** When intrusive thoughts appear, you can both label them gently - like *"That sounds like ROCD talking"*.

- **Agree on small recovery goals:** For example, *"This week I'll answer reassurance questions only once a day"*.

This part of the chapter highlights the evidence for the therapeutic approaches outlined above, showing not only how they work in practice but also the research that supports them.

Recovery from ROCD isn't just about what happens in therapy sessions - the environment you live in every day can either support healing or unintentionally reinforce OCD behaviours. A recovery-friendly environment reduces compulsions, reassurance-seeking, and avoidance, while fostering psychological safety, stability, and opportunities to practice healthy coping skills. (Olatunji et al., 2013; Fisher & Wells, 2005).

For ROCD specifically, where doubts about relationships and the need for certainty are common, the environment includes not only the individual but also partners and family members. How loved ones respond, how routines are structured, and how boundaries are maintained can make a significant difference in recovery (Soondrum et al., 2022; Twohig & Crosby, 2014).

There are further references at the back of the book, detailed under "Strategies for a Recovery-Friendly Environment", that can be read specifically in conjunction with Chapter 5.

5.4 Carer self-help – your own emotional journey

Supporting your partner through ROCD recovery takes courage and a lot of energy. As the saying goes, *"you can't pour from an empty cup"*. Here are some self-help practices for you:

- **Emotional Grounding**

  Supporting someone with ROCD can be emotionally challenging. You may feel frustration, fear, guilt, or even self-doubt as you navigate repetitive questions, reassurance-seeking, or moments of doubt and tension.

Emotional grounding is a set of practical skills and mental habits that help you stay connected to your own feelings, maintain calm, and respond from a place of stability rather than reactivity.

- **Why It Matters**

  When you stay grounded, you create a calmer environment for your partner and for yourself. ROCD thrives on uncertainty, emotional turbulence, and cycles of reassurance. If you, the partner, become anxious, reactive, or frustrated, it can unintentionally reinforce compulsive behaviours. By grounding yourself, you model calm, resilience, and emotional regulation - helping your partner feel safer and giving them space to practice coping strategies learned in therapy.

Techniques for Emotional Grounding

1. **Body Awareness:** Notice physical sensations by keeping your feet on the floor, your hands on your lap, and observing the rise and fall of your breath. Anchoring attention to the body can help interrupt spiralling thoughts.
2. **Naming Emotions:** Label your feelings (e.g., *"I feel frustrated right now"*) without judging them. Simply acknowledging emotions can reduce their intensity and help you respond thoughtfully.
3. **Mindful Breathing:** Slow, intentional breaths signal to your nervous system that you are safe. Even 5-10 breaths can reduce tension and prevent impulsive reactions.
4. **Pause Before Reacting:** Give yourself a moment before responding to your partner's doubts or questions. This brief pause allows you to choose a supportive, non-accommodating response.
5. **Focus on Values:** Remind yourself of your long-term values like compassion, patience, partnership - rather than being swept into momentary frustration or the urge to "fix" the doubt.

6. **Self-Compassion Breaks:** Acknowledge that supporting someone with ROCD is challenging and that it's okay to feel your own emotions. Treat yourself with kindness rather than self-criticism.

   Grounding is not about suppressing emotions or detaching from your partner; it's about staying present and emotionally regulated so you can respond in ways that support recovery. Over time, practising these techniques can make the day-to-day interactions calmer, reduce tension in the relationship, and protect your own well-being while your partner works through ROCD.

Journaling for reflection

Try writing down your feelings after difficult moments. Think about what triggered your stress. Did you reassure? How did it feel?

Create small joys

Even five minutes of something *that's just for you* – a walk, a song, a cup of tea outside, can help your nervous system recover. Your recovery is built on many tiny acts of self-kindness.

5.5 The Power of Psychoeducation

The most powerful thing that you can do is to learn what OCD is all about and how anxiety plays its part.

Understanding transforms fear into curiosity, and curiosity allows for change to take place.

Curiosity can be a **way of relating** rather than a strategy. When it's gentle, open, and non-directive, curiosity supports understanding and connection without trying to fix, analyse, or change anything. In that sense, it's more of an **attitude or stance** than a technique, but can be used as a strategy if there's an outcome in mind.

It may seem confusing, overwhelming, and sometimes even intimidating to learn about what OCD is for a person who does not

"Compassion and boundaries can exist together".

live with it. That is why curiosity makes such an important and compassionate starting point.

Curiosity is not about analysing yourself or others and has nothing to do with attempts at "solving" anything. It's an attitude of kindness and openness - a way of saying, *"Let me try to understand this a little better,"* without judgment, without pressure.

Psychoeducation allows you to become curious about what you are learning and, hence, remove any fear. It makes the process something safe and grounding rather than clinical or confronting. Curiosity-based psychoeducation replaces the question of *"What does that say about me?"* with a gentle query of *"I wonder what might be happening beneath the surface?"*. This shift reduces the instinct to blame yourself or others and creates space for compassion.

Curiosity is what helps make things calmer. Approaching new ideas- such as intrusive thoughts, compulsions, or the neurobiology of anxiety-with curiosity takes you out of a state of threat or overwhelm. Curiosity triggers those parts of you that want to explore, learn, and connect. It becomes easier to listen, easier to reflect, easier to hold space for someone else's experience.

Curiosity changes questions from something that might seem burdensome, like *"Why does this happen?"* - to something softer and more human - *"What might this mean for the person I care about?"*. This allows for more profound empathy because, in being curious, the urge to fix, diagnose, or even judge naturally subsides. Instead, it nurtures understanding, patience, and presence.

Curiosity lets you put new facts together in a way that feels close and important. You start to see links, join ideas, and learn how OCD hurts not only your partner but also you, who cares for them.

Curiosity is not merely a tactic- it is an empathetic pathway. Curiosity fosters gentleness, understanding, and genuine contact.

Curiosity is the gentle way to figure out what you're going through.

5.6 Creating a Joint Recovery Plan

You don't need to have a formal treatment plan, but having a shared roadmap helps you both stay aligned.

Area	Goal	Who takes the lead	Notes
Reassurance	Limit to one answer, then redirect to the coping strategy	Both	Gentle consistency is key
Exposure and Response Prevention	Face one small trigger per week	Partner	Carer provides calm encouragement
Self care	Schedule a joyful activity each day	Both	Track how it affects mood
Therapy Check-lins	Weekly reflections in progress	Partner	Carer listens without problem-solving
Relationship Time	One OCD-free evening each week	Both	Connection beyond the disorder

Even writing this plan together can shift the energy from fear to teamwork. You will notice that I have included an Exposure and Response Prevention area in the table. It is essential that you read Chapter 6 to ensure this area is safe and managed effectively.

5.7 Managing Setbacks with Compassion

Setbacks are not failures-they are just a part of getting better.

If the anxiety comes back or if a compulsion slips through, it does not mean that you or your partner are going backwards. It simply means the brain is learning new pathways and wants to revisit those old ones. Every wobble is another chance for the mind to practice resilience, to return to the skills being learned, and to make even stronger the exact pathways that need strengthening for long-term recovery.

Try this approach:

- **Pause:** don't rush in to fix.
- **Validate:** "I can see this is really hard for you".
- **Remind:** "We've been here before, and it passed then".
- **Refocus:** back to coping tools, not reassurance.

Remember, you're not aiming for perfection. You're building resilience - the ability to fall and get back up with kindness. Chapter 9 discusses more fully what setbacks can look like and what they mean.

5.8 Celebrate Progress (even the invisible kind)

In OCD recovery, the most significant victories are most often silent.

The victory of your partner withholding a question for just one moment.

The victory of a pause without reassurance.

The victory that comes when you both can share a laugh about the tricks OCD plays, rather than panic. Notice those moments. Name them! That was tough, you did it.

Hope builds up when you acknowledge it, and getting better depends a lot on having hope.

5.9 Rediscovering Connections Beyond OCD

ROCD can make your relationship feel like it's all about anxiety, but your relationship is bigger than the disorder.

Once ROCD persists for a while, it can begin to feel like an added presence in the relationship - like a demanding, intrusive individual who gets in the way of closeness, drains energy, and pulls both of you into dynamics that don't resemble who you really are. As exposure response prevention (ERP) and therapeutic work reduce the intensity of symptoms, there is often a gentle, tentative space in which partners may rediscover each other behind the noise of OCD. This reconnection is not dramatic; it doesn't occur suddenly but is made up of small moments of remembering how you used to laugh together, what your sense of humour was like, how you supported each other and that there is so much life outside doubt loops.

Reconnecting beyond OCD is allowing yourself to see the relationship in its total human entirety once again. It is an opportunity to move away from roles that the disorder created - "worrier," "reassurer," "stabiliser," "checker" - and be two people who care for one another. Partners mostly find relief in returning to everyday moments: cooking a meal together without analysing the dynamic, holding hands without searching for feelings within themselves, watching a film together without comparison or evaluation. These small acts of normalcy help bring back the natural rhythm of the relationship and remind both of you that you are more than your roles in the recovery process.

For you, reconnecting also means gently reclaiming those aspects of yourself which might have been lost to view during the time vigilance was an imperative. For your partner, reconnecting means allowing oneself to relate to the other out of interest and attentiveness rather than out of fear and watchfulness. The two movements usher in a different kind of intimacy - an intimacy that is quieter, steadier, founded in a sharing of humanness rather than a desperate quest for surety. Reconnection of this kind does not wipe away the history of struggle, but it does let the relationship breathe again, opening up space for happiness, tenderness, and quiet comfort just from being together.

5.10 Hope is Central to Getting Better

I mentioned in Step 8, that getting better depends on hope. Hope is the steady current that carries both of you through the ups and downs of ROCD recovery. It's what allows you to witness the moments

You're not just surviving this journey, you're learning a new kind of love, one that's deeper, wiser and grounded in truth.

of struggle without losing sight of progress, even when anxiety feels overwhelming, or compulsions return.

Recovery is not a straight line, and it is not about erasing every uncomfortable thought or eliminating anxiety. Instead, it is about learning to live alongside uncertainty, to tolerate discomfort, and to see that life -and love - can flourish even when the mind insists on doubt. Hope reminds both of you that change is possible, that each small step forward matters, and that even setbacks are part of the learning process, not signs of failure.

Keeping hope at the heart also embraces the broader perspective: that the goal of recovery is not perfection but freedom. Freedom to connect without constantly monitoring, freedom to be with a partner without intrusive thoughts, and freedom to feel uncertain and still stay grounded in a relationship.

When hope is present, every exposure, every moment resisting a compulsion, and every courageous attempt to face anxiety makes sense. It turns recovery from a set of chores into a shared pathway back to resilience, trust, and an even deeper, authentic connection. Hope reminds you that above all else, even when there is a lot of anxiety, life - and love - can still be rich and joyful and deeply human.

Your partner can learn to trust again. You can learn to breathe again. Your relationship can become stronger for everything you've faced together.

Every act of patience, every boundary held with love, every small step forward – these are the building blocks of healing.

You might also return to Step 6, Creating a joint recovery plan, where I introduced a sample treatment plan that you can adapt to your own needs.

One area of the plan is exposure and response prevention (ERP), and, as I explained, we'll move on in the next chapter to discuss ERP in more detail, as it is a crucial part of OCD recovery and one not to be missed. Both your own research into OCD/ROCD and your partner's therapist is likely to have discussed ERP.

Out of the Box Tools for Partners

Concept

Shared learning strengthens empathy and builds a sense of we're in this together.

Practical Tips

- Watching short psychoeducational videos on OCD together.
- Reading books or listening to podcasts about anxiety and relationships.
- Discuss what you're learning without judgement – more as team mates exploring something complex, not as 'patient and carer'.

Chapter 6

Exposure And Response Prevention (ERP)

Reason for this chapter

As I mentioned at the end of the last chapter, I included an area in the sample joint recovery plan called exposure and response prevention (ERP).

ERP is not some novelty cooked up for this book. Instead, it represents a structured method, evidence-based, that OCD specialists have long favoured as an integral part of treatment. You may have read within many OCD resources that ERP is considered the "gold standard" in managing OCD recovery. A trained therapist will guide an OCD sufferer through ERP with careful attention to safety.

The International OCD Foundation (IOCDF) includes empirical research and studies of Exposure and Response Prevention Therapy by Jon Abramowitz, PhD and states the following:

BRIEF DESCRIPTION & SUMMARY OF THE RESEARCH SUPPORT:

Exposure and response prevention (ERP) is a widely used form of cognitive-behavioural therapy (CBT) that has been the subject of numerous studies on its effects, involving thousands of adult, adolescent, and pediatric patients in countries around the world. This vast body of literature has consistently demonstrated that ERP can produce large OCD symptom reductions, which are often maintained in the long-term. On average, patients achieve a reduction of 60% of OCD symptoms, along with reductions in general anxiety, depression, interpersonal stress, and functional interference. Accordingly, ERP is recognized as a first-line, evidence-based treatment for OCD. It is considered the first-line psychological treatment due to its very strong evidence base and effectiveness in reducing symptoms and improving functioning in people with OCD.

(International OCD Foundation. (n.d.). Exposure and response prevention therapy. https://iocdf.org/ocd-treatment-guide/exposure-response-prevention/)

This chapter is here to help you, the partner, know what ERP is, why your loved one may be using it in therapy, and how you can assist without rescuing your partner or losing yourself. When both partners know the process, ERP gets safer, more effective, and much less frightening.

6.1 What ERP Is

ERP means Exposure and Response Prevention. This is a crucial element in the treatment of OCD and why I want to give it particular mention. It allows your partner to gradually confront the thoughts, situations, or feelings that trigger their anxiety while learning not to respond with any compulsion.

The triggers in the case of ROCD are usually related to the relationship itself, with intrusive thoughts like *"what if this is not the right relationship?"*, compulsive checking in on their feelings, comparison with other relationships, fear of making a mistake, doubts about love, compatibility, or even attraction.

ERP provides a structured plan to gradually and safely address these fears. In the presence of the therapist, or agreed 'homework', your partner practices letting discomfort rise and fall naturally - without performing any responses of how the original OCD was maintained, such as seeking reassurance, avoidance, or rumination.

ERP does not compel certainty.

ERP does not attempt to fix the thoughts.

ERP trains the brain and body: *"I can feel doubt and still be okay."*

6.2 Why ERP matters in ROCD

Avoidance and compulsion feed OCD. Every time your partner gives in to either reassurance-seeking or avoidance of discomfort, their mind learns that anxiety is something dangerous that has to be eliminated right away.

ERP gently breaks this cycle. Over time, your partner learns that anxiety naturally goes up and comes down, there is no need to act on thoughts, uncertainty can be tolerated, and doubt does not need to be answered.

As soon as uncertainty is welcomed, the intrusive thoughts begin to loosen their hold.

For you, the partner, understanding ERP allows you to support your partner in a way that encourages resilience- not fear, or avoidance, or dependency.

6.3 Your Role as the Partner

You have an essential role in a supportive way. The work belongs to your partner. You stand by their side, not in front of them and not instead of them.

Support, steadiness, compassion, boundaries, and emotional presence, with respect for your own needs, make this work deeply grounding. You are not obliged to guide exposures or take responsibility for their anxiety. Your role is to help create a safe emotional environment so that ERP can unfold in a manageable way. Supporting someone you love does not mean disappearing in the process. You matter too.

6.4 How ERP Works (*in everyday language*)

- **Exposure**

Preceded by purposeful confrontation of a minor trigger (e.g., an activity related to their ROCD fears), for example, your partner might read a short article about breakups, say aloud: *"It's possible I don't feel in love right now."* They would then notice the urge to check their feelings and let it be, or they might look at pictures of you both and allow comparison thoughts to come without analysing them.

Engaging in compulsions to reduce anxiety might help in the short term, but in the long run, it keeps OCD intact. Exposure means ceasing to perform and avoiding assurance seeking, checking feelings, ruminating, mentally reviewing, avoiding triggers and over-analysing their feelings.

The objective is not to lessen anxiety; it is to understand that anxiety does not have to dominate their behaviour.

As ERP is typically planned and supervised by a therapist, your function is to assist with what has been established, rather than initiating exposures or forcing advancement. Safety and feasibility are fundamental.

Methods of maintaining ERP health:

Follow your partner's lead and their therapist's.

Encourage small doable steps, not big leaps.

Provide an emotionally safe environment that does not include reassurance.

Stay calm and grounded in your own self so they can borrow from it.

Let discomfort wax and wane on its own; do not try to soothe it. End gently when the practice feels complete. Affirm courage not content: *"You handled that so bravely", "I'm here", "That took real strength."*

ERP works best when it feels like collaboration, not pressure, not force, and not monitoring.

- **ROCD ERP Partner Mistakes**

I only call these mistakes because partners care, not because anyone is doing anything wrong.

Knowing them helps keep ERP both safe and effective.

- **Accidentally giving reassurance**

Common phrases:

"You're definitely in love." "There's nothing wrong with our relationship." "It's just OCD."

Reassurance may be framed as something that helps relieve anxiety in the moment. In fact, it only strengthens ROCD in the long run.

- **Trying to take responsibility for their emotional state**

Common ways these manifest:

Tiptoeing around triggers, avoiding topics that might cause doubt, monitoring their mood, and trying to prevent exposure opportunities. This feels protective, but it sends signals to OCD: "You can't handle this."

- **Becoming overly involved in the therapy process**

For example: explaining ERP, analysing your partner's thoughts, interpreting their attachment style, reading their emotions, and determining which exposures are correct.

These decisions are between your partner and their therapist.

- **Forcing them into exposures before they're ready**

This is often done out of angst or fear.

ERP done too fast becomes unsafe and works against you, and, from my experience of working with OCD sufferers, it is throwing them into the deep end way before they are ready.

I also explain this to my clients, as they can often be keen to work with ERP, even though it sounds scary. Starting with psychoeducation and a gentle introduction to other coping strategies, I believe, is far more effective and promises longer-lasting results. Different therapists may not agree, so bear in mind that this is my opinion from my learned working practices.

- **Giving up your own needs**

You start quieting your own emotions, reducing your own personality, avoiding conflict, or taking on the household's emotional labour. Helping someone should never mean losing yourself.

Here are a couple of case examples of what giving up your own needs might look like:

Case Example 1:

"The Reassurance Spiral"

Emma is working with an OCD therapist on ERP for ROCD. During an agreed exposure, she practices sitting with the thought, "What if I made a mistake choosing Liam?", and Emma becomes distressed, turning to her partner. Emma says, "But what if it's true? What if my doubts mean something?" Liam lovingly but reflexively responds with, "It's not true. We're perfect for each other. You have anxiety." Relief flows through Emma, but it doesn't last long.

Later, the thought comes back stronger.

Liam learns to recognise that reassurance is a component of the OCD cycle, so instead, he responds differently:

Liam: "I know this is big. I'm right here with you. You don't have to work that thought out."

Emma gets support without rescue.

Liam has less pressure to "fix" her distress.

ERP gets to work better and safer.

Case Example 2:
"I Didn't Realise I Was Disappearing"

Sophie has been doing ERP with her therapist to help in the management of ROCD. Her partner, Mark, starts to shape his behaviour to avoid triggering her: by hiding romantic films, avoiding mentioning attractive people, constantly monitoring his tone, pushing down his own needs, and censoring disagreement.

During an exposure, she lets the fear "What if I'm not attracted enough to Mark?" come up and go down.

Mark sits next to her, holding tension in his body, trying to be "perfectly calm."

Over weeks, Mark begins to feel depleted and invisible. With guidance, he learns to remain present without over-functioning.

Mark: "I care about you deeply, and I'm here. But I also need to stay connected to myself. We can face this together without me disappearing."

Sophie learns she can tolerate her fears without needing Mark to erase himself.

Mark learns that supporting her does not mean silencing his own life force.

There will be more examples, but these two, in particular, are commonly practised.

Some closing thoughts on ERP

ERP is integral to the recovery from OCD, initiated and supervised by competent therapists who are experienced in the safe pacing of exposures. Your role as the partner is just as important, but different. You can provide emotional warmth with soft boundaries, supportive but non-rescuing, present but not taking on their anxiety and holding onto yourself while walking beside them.

Recovery from ROCD is a joint effort, but proper and healthy recovery can only take place when both individuals in the relationship are permitted to stay intact.

Chapter 7

Reclaiming Yourself

Now that we've touched on exposure response prevention exercises for your partner, this chapter is written to help you gently turn the spotlight back onto your own well-being, that part that often gets lost when you're supporting your partner through ROCD.

If you don't give yourself a chance to refuel, then your relationship can start to feel like survival rather than connection.

When you live alongside someone with ROCD, you learn to read moods, anticipate needs, and attempt to soften sharp edges. YOU adapt! You can adapt so well that you start to forget where you end and where the OCD begins.

Your well-being matters as much as your partner's, so you might find it easy to overlook some of these tell-tale signs:

- Feeling like you're always on call.
- Walking on eggshells to avoid triggering your partner's anxiety.
- Neglecting your own hobbies or friendships.
- Feeling guilty when you take time for yourself.
- Resenting the condition, but feeling guilty for that too.

These reactions are entirely normal. They are signs of compassion fatigue, not a lack of love.

Try to remember, fatigue doesn't mean you are failing. It's a signal you've been trying hard for too long without enough rest.

7.1 Permitting Yourself to Have Feelings

I'm sure you sometimes feel under pressure to stay endlessly patient, calm, and strong, but is that sustainable? You are likely to have moments of frustration, grief, and even anger. That is ok! These feelings don't make you an unkind, uncaring person – they make you human.

Instead of being your own judge and jury, see these feelings as signals instead:

- **Anger** – might be telling you that a boundary has been crossed.
- **Sadness** – might be asking you to acknowledge a loss – of ease, spontaneity, or the relationship you once had.
- **Exhaustion** – might be a quiet plea for rest.

When you allow your feelings to exist, they move through you instead of staying stuck.

The Oxygen Mask Rule

If you've ever travelled on an aeroplane, you've probably heard this: *"Put on your own oxygen mask before helping others"*.

It works perfectly here and is a gentle reminder that you can't pour calm into someone who is already anxious if you are already running on empty. It's more helpful to your partner to try to remain steady and grounded. Taking care of yourself isn't selfish. It's essential for the two of you.

A little takeaway in this chapter for you:

Words that begin with self - like self-care, self-respect, and self-compassion are often mistaken as suggesting that turning toward yourself means turning away from others.

To care for yourself is in no way selfish. It is a tender way to pay respect to that very self which moves through this world every day carrying hopes, burdens, and responsibilities. These acts whisper reminders that you do have needs, that you can permit yourself to speak them, to set boundaries that must be respected and to allow yourself to be cared for by your own hands in your own time.

You will naturally come into a grounded place where you will find yourself more able to care for others as warmly and lovingly as you care for yourself.

7.2 Reclaiming small moments of inner calm

OCD thrives on uncertainty, so caring for your partner can make you feel like life is unpredictable. One of the most healing things you can do is introduce some grounding in your own life to nurture yourself.

Here are some nurturing ideas:

- **Morning ritual:** Start the day with something that's just for you – a walk, your favourite song/music, journaling, or a cup of tea.
- **Digital boundaries:** Permit yourself to switch off your phone for a while without guilt.
- **Mini escapes:** 15 minutes outside can reset your nervous system.
- **Creative outlet:** Paint, write, garden, move, cook – anything that connects you with yourself again.

These moments don't have to be too big. They have to be yours.

"……We can't practice compassion with other people if we can't treat ourselves kindly".

- Brene Brown

7.3 What Self-Compassion Looks Like

Self-compassion isn't about indulgence; it's about honesty. It's saying to yourself – *"This is hard, and I'm doing my best"*. (Neff, n.d.)

Here's a simple exercise you can do to demonstrate self-compassion:

- Place a hand on your heart.
- Breathe slowly.
- Say gently: *"This is a moment of difficulty. Others feel like this too. I choose to be kind to myself"*.

Self-compassion is something I always bring attention to in a 1:1 therapy session with an ROCD sufferer or their partner. Self-compassion seems to be lacking in most people's lives, mainly because they consider it self-indulgent, as I mentioned in the "take-away" above. It is much easier for our inner critical voice to shout the loudest for attention and work its hardest to show our "not good enough-ness". If you're interested in exploring self-compassion further, I strongly suggest Kirsten Neff, PhD – she has various books and workbooks in this area- or Brené Brown – both are available through most reputable retailers. The example above is just one form of self-compassion, and, if you are reading this alongside "ROCD, *Is it a thing?*", is also discussed in more detail.

7.4 The Importance of Connection

You might feel, as many people do, that no one understands what it's like to live with ROCD in the house, so caring can feel very isolating.

If possible, work with a therapist who understands OCD and caregiver burnout, so you can be heard - really heard - as this can be profoundly healing. I know it's difficult when people don't understand the complexities of OCD, but try to reach out to a trusted family member anyway, not for fixing, but someone who listens. There are also support groups online.

It isn't selfish to look after yourself. It's nourishing".

7.5 When it's Time to Seek Your Own Support

Sometimes, despite your best efforts, you might find yourself overwhelmed - anxious, tearful, or even numb. Take this as a sign that you may need extra support.

It is okay to seek therapy for yourself. Since I wrote "ROCD, *Is it a thing?*", my ongoing therapy work with ROCD sufferers, and the growing impact of my own social media content around OCD awareness, it has become increasingly apparent that carers/partners need empathetic support as much as their loved ones. Many therapists who specialise in working with people with OCD offer support for the carers/partners as well.

Therapy for carers isn't about complaining about your partner - it's about learning coping strategies, boundaries and self-understanding. Strategies, I hope this book will offer, alongside therapy or as a self-help guide.

7.6 Reconnecting With Your Own Identity

Caring for your partner with ROCD naturally means pouring large amounts of emotional energy into efforts at support, soothing fears, and trying to keep the relationship feeling safe. Over time, this can unthinkingly draw you away from your own identity and what your interests are, what your values are, where joy is found, and even what your sense of self-worth might be.

Getting back to who you are is not some fancy thing; it's an essential way to ground. When you have a good inner anchor that brings you up with patience and compassion rather than tiredness or overwhelm, self-care keeps you in touch not just with your partner but also with your own inner life, which deserves as much kindness and attention.

Reconnecting with your own identity also gently recalibrates the relationship. ROCD can set up patterns, like reassurance-seeking or giving, that become so emotionally draining on both ends. When you

Your partner is on a recovery journey – and you deserve one too!

reconnect with your needs and interests, you start practising and then modelling emotional autonomy. You show that it is okay for everybody to have their own space, passion, and grounding practices. It does not pull you away from your partner; instead, it builds the foundation beneath you so you can be present without losing yourself. In nurturing your identity, you give your partner something else more valuable - stability and authenticity, plus a better relationship rhythm that makes both of you feel secure and whole.

A simple self-check is:

- What used to bring you joy that you no longer do?
- What parts of yourself have gone quiet since the ROCD took centre stage?

Write those answers down. Then choose one *small thing* to reintroduce this week.

7.7 Building a Supportive Inner Voice

Earlier in this chapter, I mentioned that our inner critical voice shouts louder than any other. Have you noticed how you speak to yourself?

When you're the partner of someone living with ROCD, your inner voice becomes an integral part of how you cope, stay resilient and show up with compassion.

A harsh inner critic drains your emotional resilience, especially when you're already navigating cycles of reassurance, doubt, or emotional intensity. If your self-talk is filled with blame, pressure, or perfectionism, it becomes much harder to stay grounded - you may start believing you're "not doing enough," "causing the problem," or "failing" your partner.

An encouraging inner voice will help keep you centred and preserve the relationship. When people speak to themselves with compassion, they can respond to their partner from a place of calm rather than from anxiety, self-doubt, or emotional flooding. The way your internal landscape looks is how you come across externally. An encouraging, nurturing inner voice helps you create better boundaries, communicate more clearly, and maintain emotional equilibrium. It does not allow you to over-extend. It does not allow you to try to "fix" everything which is unfixable most of the time with ROCD and leads to exhaustion.

Encouraging a more positive inner voice helps you build an inner home, a spot where you can relax, renew, and recall that you are trying your best. The care you show yourself will flow outwards to others, making the bond safer, more stable, and easier to keep.

Remember, you're looking to shift from self-criticism to inner encouragement.

Here are some ideas:

Old Inner Critical Voice	New Encouraging Voice
"I should not feel this way".	"It's okay to feel what I feel".
"I'm not doing enough".	"I'm doing what I can today".
"I can't handle this".	"Right now, this is hard, but it will pass".

Your internal voice sets the tone for how you experience everything else.

Let it be kind!

7.8 The Ripple Effect of Self-Care

Self-care tends to foster a healthier emotional climate in the relationship. By practising self-care, setting soft boundaries, and acknowledging personal needs, it is hoped that your partner feels more secure and is encouraged and inspired to do the same and reflect that energy.

Obviously, we can't guarantee this. Everybody is different, everybody has their past, and everybody has their habits. It might inspire others to do better by taking care of themselves, but it won't force them to improve. To put it better, self-care builds your strength, and most of the time, that strength enhances the relationship.

A Simple Evening Reflection

Here's a small ritual you can try before bed:

Close your eyes and ask yourself these three questions:

- *What went well today?*
- *What was difficult?*
- *What do I need tomorrow?*

This can help keep you connected to yourself – and is also a reminder that your needs matter too.

Supporting a partner with ROCD can make communication feel delicate, as though every word must be measured to avoid triggering distress. It's understandable to feel like you're walking on eggshells, unsure of how to express yourself without making things more complicated, and, as we explored at the beginning of the chapter, how you might adapt your own behaviours, so as not to rock the boat.

"Out of the box" Tool for Partners

Concept

Loving someone with ROCD can quietly teach you to shrink, to be careful, to hold more than your share.

A ***compassionate, quiet rebellion*** is choosing yourself in small, gentle ways without turning away from the relationship.

Practical tips:

- **Pausing before offering reassurance**, even when it feels uncomfortable
- **Stepping back from fixing or explaining**, and letting anxiety pass on its own.
- **Taking space or rest when you need it**, without apologising

This isn't selfish. It's self-compassion.

A compassionate, quiet rebellion says:

I can love you and still take up space.

Choose one small moment this week to come back to yourself.

You don't have to disappear to stay connected.

In the next chapter, I'll share how to communicate with your partner in ways that strengthen connection rather than strain it - offering you practical, compassionate tools to speak openly, stay grounded, and build a safer emotional space for both of you.

Chapter 8

Talking Without Feeding the OCD

Communication in a relationship creates a connection.

Healthy communication involves sharing feelings, needs, and boundaries without repeatedly seeking confirmation that everything is "okay."

Asking the same question in different ways is a sign that communication has crossed into OCD-driven territory. Other signs include feeling an urgent need to get certainty and believing the relationship is in danger unless a specific response is given. You might notice conversations that loop, or you might notice that your own anxiety gets higher, or you feel like you have to provide the "perfect" answer to calm your partner's fears.

A simple *"Do you love me?"* may be the honest vulnerability of expression, or it may be the beginning of a reassurance compulsion. You might have begun picking up on little cues. You might notice your partner reaching for reassurance more often - not inquiring of you but trying to quiet the sudden waves of doubt that ROCD can bring.

- Sometimes, ordinary talk seems laden, as though a simple remark has caused concern in them which you did not mean.
- They may require you to clarify something, not due to lack of clarity, but because their apprehension is seeking an unseen meaning.

- You will notice the same worry coming back with different words; this shows that their mind is circling and not that they do not believe your first answer.
- They might suddenly read too much into your tone or timing. Anxiety makes little things seem like big signals.
- They might ask significant questions in quiet times about your feelings or the state of the two of you. This comes more from a need for safety than any real worry about you.
- Some discussions might repeat themselves, not out of distrust for you, but because their minds nudge them toward reassurance. They might look uneasy if matters seem unresolved, just needing to be sure they haven't by chance harmed you or put the bond at risk.

8.1 The Pause

Before you answer questions like this, take a second to ask yourself:

"Am I responding to my partner or their anxiety?".

Learning to pause before answering gives you the choice to step out of the cycle. This doesn't mean you are withholding love. It's more about deciding which part of the conversation you want to feed - the relationship or the OCD.

8.2 Communicating with empathy and boundaries

Words spoken with kindness and firmness at the same time, may be something like,

- *"I know this feels scary. I don't want to give you an answer that makes the worry louder".*
- *"It sounds like the OCD is telling you a story again. How can I support you in sitting with that?".*

- *"I love you. I am here. That is not something I can be reassuring about right now".*
- *"Let us notice what it is saying and try not to solve it".*

These phrases not only validate the emotion, but they name the OCD and set a gentle boundary.

8.3 Listening without fixing

Simply *listening* is the most healing thing you can do, not to agree or solve, but to listen, to validate.

Active listening calms the nervous system. It's saying, "*I see you*". *You're safe here*. When people feel secure, they feel more able to face their fears.

You might try saying:

- *"That sounds exhausting".*
- *"I can hear how much you are struggling with that thought".*
- *"You don't have to have an answer right now".*

8.4 Expressing your own needs

Good communication isn't just one-sided. You have the right to speak your own truth, too.

You can also say things like:

- *"I want to talk about this, but I need to know it's not reassurance-seeking".*
- *"I feel anxious when we go round the same question. Can we take a break?".*
- *"I love you, and I also need space sometimes to look after myself".*

When such words are said with softness and honesty, the dynamic shifts from 'you versus me' to 'us versus the problem'. Expressing individual needs in conversation with an ROCD partner matters, not only for personal well-being, but also for the well-being of

"ROCD is loud – but you don't have to be. Calm, steady presence is powerful".

your relationship. By communicating boundaries, preferences, and emotions, you present to your partner something real and consistent with which they can interact, much better than the uncertainty they have to offer.

Direct conversation prevents emotions from building and prevents confusion from setting in. It breaks the comforting behaviours gently because the narrative has now shifted from *'how do I comfort them'* to *'how do we show up for each other with truth?'*

To an ROCD partner, hearing your needs expressed calmly can be grounding; it brings them back to a conscious level that the relationship is a two-way connection and not a performance they should be rating continuously. Speaking up firmly and with compassion shows you model healthy emotional balance, which creates space for both of you to speak from your authentic selves rather than from fear.

8.5 When Conversations Get Stuck

With even your best intentions, there may be times when you get pulled back into old patterns. That's okay. Try a reset when you notice you're both getting stuck.

- Agree to stop the conversation.
- Name what is happening, like, *"I think we've got caught in an OCD loop"*.
- Take a short break – a walk, a drink of water, some deep breaths to break the cycle.
- Agree to return later with calmer energy.

Stopping mid-loop does not mean avoiding. It means choosing to re-engage when you are both grounded enough to do it well.

8.6 Nurturing your everyday connection

Not every conversation needs to be about OCD or recovery. One of the healthiest things you can do is to "protect" your everyday talk - the general, simple stuff that's a reminder of why you're together.

Talk about your hobbies and interests, your friends, and plans for the weekend. Laugh and share small moments. The more you can feed ordinary life, the more minor OCD feels in your shared world.

8.7 Using Check-Ins

You might find it helpful to schedule brief, structured check-ins. This can help stop ROCD from hijacking every moment. ROCD likes to suck the joy out of almost everything.

No couple gets it right, especially with anxiety in the mix. What matters most is a willingness to repair, to check in after a misfire, to apologise when needed, to reaffirm care. Repair builds emotional safety and shows that conflict doesn't equal catastrophe. For someone with ROCD, this is an essential message.

Pick one 15-minute slot per day, in which to talk about anxiety or progress toward success. This will keep the lines of communication open but confined, creating a boundary that feels safe for both of you. If reassurance questions are asked outside of this time, you can gently say, *"Let's save that for our check-in"*.

Speaking in the language of "team" can be very grounding when you are going through ROCD. Words such as *"Let's work it out together"* or *"We're on the same side"* can reorient communication from anxious interrogation to connection and shared problem-solving. It brings back to the consciousness of both of you that ROCD is the problem, and not your relationship.

8.8 When professional help joins the conversation

If you or your partner are in therapy, it might be helpful to attend a session occasionally, if your therapy agreement allows it. This might help align on each other's treatment plans so that everyone is going in the same direction and growth becomes a shared language.

8.9 Closing the day with connection

Sharing a hug, or something that made you both laugh today, or a simple *"thank you for today"*, are small moments to hold. These moments of peace remind the two of you that under the anxiety, there is still love - that is solid, imperfect and real.

These are some tools for talking that protect your relationship, whilst supporting recovery.

There may well be times when progress feels slow, fear sneaks back in, and when you, the partner/carer, feel like you're starting all over again.

This is where compassion, for both of you, comes into its own again and is more powerful than any quick fix. I may well be boring the pants off you for mentioning compassion by now, but I can't stress enough, or put more strongly, the importance of compassion during OCD management and recovery.

"Out of the box" Tool for Partners

Concept

The Unfinished Sentence

OCD pulls conversations toward certainty and completion -answers, explanations and endings.

One way to step out of that pull is to leave the sentence unfinished, creating space for uncertainty without feeding it, and breaking the compulsion without confrontation. It can subtly retrain the nervous system to tolerate "not finishing". This is a slightly unconventional approach, but very aligned with talking without feeding OCD.

Practical Tips:

When the conversation starts to loop, respond and then stop before resolving it - not abruptly, not defensively - just gently unfinished.

Examples:

- *"I hear how urgent this feels, and right now I'm noticing..."*
- *"This feels like one of those moments where we could keep going, or we could..."*
- *"I care about you, and I'm choosing to..."*

Then you stop.

As we've explored, gentle communication and clear boundaries can help maintain your connection, even in the midst of ROCD.

But change doesn't always feel straightforward, and there may be moments when progress seems slow or even like it's gone backwards. That's normal - it doesn't mean the work isn't helping. In the next chapter, we'll look at what it can feel like when things get stuck, and how to respond in ways that keep you and your relationship moving forward, with patience and compassion.

Chapter 9

Setbacks and Feeling Stuck

Recovery from OCD is rarely straightforward.

You know that one moment, when you feel like you've turned a corner, and whoosh, the same old fears come knocking again. It can be accompanied by a mix of frustration, exhaustion and guilt, and you end up asking yourself, *"Why is this happening again? What am I doing wrong?"*.

The truth is, you're not doing anything wrong.

It's essential to understand what setbacks in ROCD can mean, where they might come from and why self-compassion is massively helpful towards recovery.

It may help to hold this idea in your mind that setbacks are not always signals to change direction.

Usually, they are invitations to slow down, reduce pressure and respond with calmness rather than urgency. What follows builds on this, not by offering ways to avoid difficulty but to help you stay grounded when it arises.

9.1 What ROCD setbacks are

When your partner has ROCD, setbacks can be confusing and painful for both of you.

Your partner may suddenly seem unsure, distant, or emotionally withdrawn, even if nothing in the relationship has changed.

A setback is not a change in love or commitment. It's a temporary surge of anxiety that hijacks how your partner experiences their thoughts and feelings.

What's happening during a setback

ROCD affects the brain's alarm system.

During a setback, that alarm goes off again, even though there is no real danger.

Your partner isn't discovering a new and hidden truth about the relationship. Their brain is reacting to stress, uncertainty, closeness, or exhaustion by creating doubt and fear.

It's like how a panic attack convinces someone they're in danger even when they're safe. The fear feels real, but it isn't accurate.

9.2 Why your partner may become distant or conflicted

During a setback, your partner may:

- overanalyse their feelings or yours.
- question things they usually don't about themselves or you.
- feel emotionally numb or disconnected from yourself.
- worry they're "leading you on" or the other way round.
- feel guilty for not feeling certain.

This isn't intentional. Your partner's mind has gone back to trying to fix anxiety by searching for certainty, something no relationship can ever provide.

9.3 Why reassurance and pressure to talk it through make it worse

As you've learned, when your partner panics, they often feel an urgent need to "figure things out."

If they're pushed to talk it through, make decisions, or explain their doubts, the anxiety intensifies.

Reassurance may help briefly, but it teaches the brain that the fear is important - so it comes back stronger.

What works better is calmness and compassion, rather than treating the fear as a crisis.

9.4 Why compassion matters more than logic

During a setback, logic doesn't reach your partner the same way it usually would. The nervous system has returned to survival mode.

Here comes the "compassion" part again!

Compassion helps by:

- calming the fear response.
- reducing shame and guilt.
- helping your partner stay grounded instead of spiralling.
- allowing the setback to pass naturally.

..... and applying all the above to yourself as well.

A simple understanding, without trying to fix or interpret the thoughts, can shorten the duration of a setback.

9.5 What an ROCD setback does not mean

As a gentle reminder, a setback does not mean:

- the relationship is actually failing.
- love has gone.
- you or your partner must make a decision.
- your relationship is lacking in honesty.
- the doubts are actually "real".

It means your partner, or yourself, is overwhelmed internally and needs safety, not answers.

9.6 What helps during a setback

What works best is patience, emotional steadiness, not demanding certainty, not pushing for explanations, and treating it as temporary. Even a quiet presence, acting normal and being grounded can be profoundly reassuring without feeding the anxiety.

Your partner might bounce back faster this time, or you might find you're calmer when the anxiety spikes. That's called growth, even if it doesn't feel like it in the moment.

Staying grounded when anxiety rises

When your partner's anxiety rises, it can be easy to get pulled back into the emotional storm.

Here are a few steps to keep yourself steady:

- **Pause before responding** - give yourself a breath or two before speaking. This brief circuit breaker stops you from automatically slipping into reassurance-giving.
- **Notice what's yours and what's theirs** - by not taking ownership of their distress, you can still feel empathy.
- **Physically anchor yourself** -remind your body that you are safe, even if the atmosphere feels tense -by touching something solid as a grounding technique -for example, the back of a chair or stamping your feet on the ground.
- **Don't try to be logical - try to be calm** - a quiet voice and body language do far more than perfect words.

The most important thing to remember

Setbacks are part of recovery and not signs that your relationship isn't working. Each time a setback is met with calm instead of panic, the brain slowly learns that doubt is not dangerous. Over time, they become less intense and less frequent.

9.7 If you feel hopeless

Some days might feel heavy, and you may well feel tired of always being the strong one, of tiptoeing about, or of wondering if things will ever change.

Hopelessness is a natural part of caregiving because caring deeply while having limited control is emotionally exhausting. When you support someone who is struggling, you can do everything "right" and still not see immediate change, which can make effort feel invisible and progress feel uncertain.

That constant balance between staying strong, being patient, and managing your own emotions can feel like it's draining your hope over time. Feeling hopeless doesn't mean you're failing or giving up. It means you're human and being affected by sustained stress, love, and responsibility without guaranteed relief.

In these moments, don't fight the feeling.

Sit with it.

Say to yourself, *"This is hard right now. I don't have to have hope this minute – I just have to rest."*

9.8 Permitting yourself to take little breaks

When things feel stuck, it can be tempting to make the relationship all about the ROCD, by analysing it, reading about it and talking about it constantly. This can often make ROCD feel even heavier.

Try to build even small moments of your "normal" into life:

- Watch a show together.
- Cook a favourite meal.
- Go for a walk without discussing the ROCD.
- Play with a pet, listen to your favourite music, or share a joke.

These are healing moments and not distractions. They can remind both of you that there is life beyond ROCD.

"Hope doesn't always look like bright optimism; sometimes it's just refusing to give up on gentleness."

9.9 Keep an eye out for the quiet wins

When recovery feels slow, it's helpful to name the progress you can't see. Maybe your partner didn't ask for reassurance today, even though you could tell they wanted to. Perhaps you didn't raise your voice during a stressful conversation. Maybe you both managed to laugh after a long, complicated week. If you can, write these things down. Even if you think your win is tiny, it's proof that growth is happening beneath the surface.

Sometimes you find some surprising little moments of growth that only make sense in hindsight.

9.10 When it feels that intimacy and connection suffer

Your relationship can feel strained during long-term anxiety struggles, and, commonly, intimacy and connection can feel affected.

This doesn't mean the love between you has disappeared. It means you are both exhausted.

You can rebuild closeness slowly by:

- Showing small gestures of affection without pressurising.
- Checking in in an honest and gentle way.
- Sharing experiences that aren't therapy related.

Think of connection as something to rebuild, and not something you fix overnight.

9.11 Doing less instead of more

Instead of rushing in to make your partner's anxiety go away, focus on a balanced presence.

- *"I'm here".*
- *"I believe you can handle this".*
- *"You're not alone".*

When you step back to support your partner without over-functioning, you give them room to build their own resilience, which is the ultimate goal of recovery.

Sometimes the most loving act is to do less, rather than trying to fix, soothe or organise.

9.12 Special days and temporary spikes

Setbacks in ROCD rarely arrive without context.

They can appear suddenly around moments like anniversaries, holidays, birthdays, family gatherings, plans, or quiet milestones, which end up feeling overshadowed by doubt, distance, or distress.

When this happens, it's easy to interpret it as a setback in the relationship itself, painful for you and confusing for your partner.

In reality, these moments are often predictable, nervous anxiety moments, not signs of failure. ROCD tends to flare when something feels emotionally loaded or symbolic, as special days and dates carry meaning, expectation, and often an unspoken sense of "this matters". For a mind already wired to scan for certainty, these moments can amplify your partner's anxiety rather than joy. The spike isn't because the relationship is wrong, it's because the relationship matters.

This distinction is important for you because, without it, these episodes can feel personal, rejecting, or deeply discouraging.

Why these can be especially hard

Special occasions invite reflection. They often come with questions such as *"Am I feeling enough?", "Is this how it's supposed to feel?"* or *"What does this say about our future?"* Even when these questions are not spoken aloud, they can create intense internal pressure.

As you've learned, ROCD thrives on urgency and meaning. When a day feels significant, the mind may test that moment for clarity, certainty or a particular emotional response. When that response doesn't arrive naturally, doubt rushes in to fill the gap. The reason is that when your partner is testing themselves for the "right" answer, their mind is already worried, so anxiety follows.

These spikes are not usually about the relationship. Stress, fatigue, illness, life transitions, family dynamics, or emotional vulnerability can create them, and sadly, since it is the relationship that gets blamed for the discomfort, it is there that the spill happens.

It is worth noting here that hormonal transitions can significantly influence ROCD symptoms. Many women report spikes during times of fluctuation such as perimenopause, menopause, post-partum, premenstrual phases, and across the menstrual cycle, likely due to the impact of shifting oestrogen and progesterone on mood, anxiety, and cognitive processing. Research into the hormonal-OCD connection is ongoing, but growing evidence suggests these biological changes can heighten vulnerability to intrusive thoughts and doubt during sensitive periods.

Content rarely matters, even though it feels that way; only the meaning and priority rating applied to the content cause the distress.

Keep your focus on patterns, as ROCD spikes most often share a particular quality: an urgency to "figure things out"; repetitive questioning or reassurance-seeking; heightened analysis of feelings or connection; emotional withdrawal; irritability; and restlessness. It feels like a decision needs to be made right away.

A genuine relationship problem usually invites conversation about specific issues.

This is not about labelling or invalidating worry. It's about paying attention to how something comes across, not only what is being said. Tone, timing, and intensity often speak far louder than words ever can.

When a spike falls at a meaningful date or event, it can be helpful to gently hold that context in mind, even if it isn't named out loud.

What can you do?

You don't need to be perfect in supporting your partner through these moments, or expect endless patience, or sacrifice your own emotional reality. Calmness and perspective are key:

State the pattern, not the problem. Rather than engage with the doubt itself, note its timing: *"This feels like it's coming up around a lot of pressure today."* You can then shift the focus away from labelling the relationship as problematic while still validating the distress.

- **Resist the reassurance cycle (kindly):** repeated reassurance unintentionally strengthens ROCD. That doesn't mean you withdraw affection or become cold. It means you offer presence without feeding the ROCD loop. Say something like: *"I can see how uncomfortable this feels. I'm here with you but I don't think answering that question again will help right now"*.
- **Lower the emotional temperature:** during spikes, clarity rarely comes from talking more. It often comes from grounding - rest, distraction, routine, or simply letting the moment pass. Suggesting a walk, a meal, or a change of focus can be far more supportive than another relationship discussion.
- **Hold your own experience of the relationship:** supporting your partner does not require you to doubt your own feelings, memories or sense of connection. You are allowed to trust your own experience, even when your partner cannot access theirs in the moment.

  This is especially important on special days, when you can feel erased or sidelined by the disorder.
- **Compassionate reflection and reframing:** when things settle, it can be helpful to reflect, *"That was a hard moment, and it happened around a meaningful day. That tells us something, not about us, but about how relationship stressors show up."* This turns the experience into information rather than evidence of failure.

Spikes around special days are not steps backwards. They are often signs that something meaningful has stirred vulnerability, expectation, or fear. Seen through this lens, they become part of the landscape of ROCD rather than proof that progress has been lost.

Your goal is not to eliminate these moments, but to recognise them as temporary states rather than lasting truths.

9.13 When to encourage professional help

It's time to reach out for professional support if your partner's setback is lasting weeks, or if you find your partner withdrawing, avoiding life or showing signs of depression. You can also seek support to help you manage your boundaries and prevent burnout.

Encouragement works best when it's delivered with care, not in a forced way.

You might say, *"I think you've been carrying a lot lately. How would you feel about checking in with your therapist again?"*

9.14 Preventing your own burnout

You can't prevent every relapse, but you can prevent yourself from burning out along the way by making space to revisit your own hobbies, friends, and a spiritual or creative life that's not dependent on your partner's progress.

Remember, you are a whole person, not a supporting character in their story.

Sometimes, when partners/carers start reclaiming their own lives, the person with OCD paradoxically feels freer to do the same.

When you are tired, try offering some kindness to yourself with this gentle mantra: *"We've been here before. We know the way out. This is not the end, it's just another bend in the road"*.

Keep this sentence close. It's both true and grounding.

Setbacks are a natural part of any journey. Those moments where old patterns resurface, or progress feels slow, don't erase the work you've already done. Each challenge you face is also an opportunity to notice what strategies have helped, what feels supportive, and where you might need a gentler approach.

"We've been here before. We know the way out. This is not the end, it's just another bend in the road.

"Out of the box" Tool for Partners

Concept:

OCD's Note (and Your Response)

As I explained, setbacks can often spike on high-expectation days - birthdays, anniversaries, or emotionally charged moments. Writing from OCD's perspective helps you step outside the loop.

Practical Tips:

1. Write one sentence **from OCD** (e.g.*"They might not care enough. You need proof."*).
2. Write one grounded line **from yourself** - not reassurance, just your calm, compassionate response.
3. Notice the space this creates - you're present without feeding the loop.

Why It Helps:

It makes confusing setbacks tangible, keeps you grounded, and lets you stay connected to your partner without being pulled into compulsive reassurance.

In the next chapter, we'll bring everything together, weaving the ideas and tools you've explored so far into a cohesive approach that you can adapt to your own relationship, helping you move forward with confidence and compassion.

Chapter 10

Bringing It All Together Through Self-Help

As you have learned and understood so far, the journey to recovery is not all smooth and, at times, has probably felt a bit like a hike up a mountain.

Those steep climbs, unexpected turns, moments of doubt, and times when the path ahead has been hidden by fog. If it were a real hike, you wouldn't have started climbing without your map, supplies, and a basic understanding of the terrain you're crossing.

Therefore, you need insight into what lies ahead before meaningful progress can set in. Knowing what you are up against reduces confusion, self-directed anger, and fear, and helps you respond intentionally rather than instinctively.

In the absence of such knowledge, it becomes very easy to read symptoms as facts, and backward steps as failures, or to move unintentionally in ways that make the climb even more difficult.

For partners and carers, this has meant:

- **Learning about ROCD and its mechanisms**

As you have read, understanding how intrusive thoughts, doubt, reassurance-seeking, and avoidance compulsions fuel the cycle is essential. Many compulsions don't look obvious or dramatic; they can be subtle, relational, and easily mistaken for "normal" conversations, and checking in with these can unintentionally reinforce the cycle.

- **Recognising your own emotional responses**

You've also learned that ROCD doesn't only affect the person experiencing it.

It can pull you into feelings of guilt, fear, frustration, sadness, or even resentment. Becoming aware of your own internal experience helps you respond more thoughtfully, rather than being driven by the urge to fix, soothe, or prove something in the moment.

- **Acceptance of roles and limits**

However much you love your partner, however much you want to help, you cannot do the work of recovery on your own. They have work to do in facing uncertainty and discomfort, and your job is different but equally important: supporting recovery without getting roped into the cycle. Acceptance isn't about letting go; it's about seeing what is and what isn't within your control.

When both of you share the understanding that compulsions, however they show up, only provide short-term relief at a long-term cost, the dynamic begins to shift.

Healing involves learning to sit with uncertainty and discomfort rather than trying to escape or neutralise it. With this shared perspective, you're no longer climbing unthinkingly, but moving with a new awareness and intention, sitting in the knowledge that discomfort is part of the ascent, and not a sign you're on the wrong path. With this understanding, you're in a great position to make progress up that mountain.

10.1 Building a Shared Vision

In Chapter 8, we looked at adding structure to any jointly agreed ROCD conversations. Sit down together and talk about what recovery looks like for each of you. You can ask questions like:

- *"What would life look like if OCD wasn't running the show?"*
- *"What would we be doing more of?"*
- *"What small steps could we take to get closer to that?"*

This conversation shifts the focus from what's going wrong to what's possible.

Each of you write your answers down as a discussion point. Even a few sentences can become a compass if things go off track.

See recovery as a shared project, rather than a solo mission.

10.2 Creating Daily Anchors

Knowing the terrain means setting daily anchors for yourself and your partner. With ROCD in the picture, days can easily be consumed by doubt, emotional fluctuations, and an urgent search for certainty.

These daily anchors help to function within a values framework, protecting boundaries as reference points - small, intentional, values-led practices that help settle your nervous system and reconnect both of you to life outside of the ROCD cycle.

They don't make anxiety go away or prove anything about the relationship, but they give structure, grounding, and some sense of continuity, however chaotic your internal experiences may feel.

For your partner, daily anchors could include planned exposure or response prevention work, a quick mindfulness or grounding practice, journaling about values rather than feelings, keeping up non-negotiable routines like exercise to show self-care continues, and making space for creative time and regular meals. These anchors help convey that life goes on even in the face of doubt and that discomfort can be borne for a while without immediate resolution.

All of these strategies are shared in my book, "ROCD, *Is it a thing?*", and can also be what serves you well in the fight not to succumb to ROCD. Protected time with friends and/or hobbies, therapy or support spaces of your own, movement or relaxation practices, and having clear boundaries around reassurance conversations seem to unstick the energy and are equally important. Values-led practices drop anchors that help you stay emotionally resourced, reduce the pull to rescue or reassure, and prevent your own world from shrinking around the disorder.

When the two of you deliberately set such anchors in everyday life, the relationship will not be so much overtaken by ROCD as grounded in shared values. Anchors do not take away the climb, but they provide firm places to step on the way up. They remind you that even on bad days, there is still a seat to sit on for a while and gather your bearings before heading out once more.

Think about how you can weave your values into everyday life.

10.3 Managing Reassurance Together

You've noticed how reassurance often sneaks in under the radar, disguised as repeated questions like *"Do you still love me?"*, *"Are we really okay?"*, or *"Did that mean something?"* These questions seem on the surface to be relational and reasonable, but when ROCD drives them, they rapidly become part of a loop - briefly soothing the anxiety, while strengthening the doubt and increasing the urge to ask again. When you work as a team rather than from opposite sides of the anxiety, you can begin to interrupt these patterns.

You could create a clear and compassionate "Reassurance Agreement". What this shared understanding typically sounds like is: *"Whenever you request reassurance, I'll gently point out to you that this is your ROCD speaking. I'll give you emotional support and offer my presence, but I will not give any answers or provide certainty."* The purpose is not withholding love or care; rather, it is to separate the act of loving from the compulsion of needing certainty.

This is you, warmly acknowledging your partner's pain, giving a hug, or saying, *"I can see you are anxious right now. I am with you,"* without providing the reassurance that momentarily quiets the fear but, in the end, strengthens it. For your partner, this becomes an opportunity to notice the urge, name it as anxiety and practice sitting with discomfort rather than seeking immediate relief.

Over time, this puts both of you in a different frame of mind about what reassurance is. It is no longer looked at as proof or evidence of love or safety but rather as a signal that anxiety is active and should be met with compassion and groundedness - it requires a skilful response, not certainty-seeking.

With consistency, trust starts to replace constant reassurance, allowing some new, healthier support to come into play.

10.4 Cultivating tolerance for uncertainty

Every time you choose to sit with your partner through their uncertainty, rather than explain or provide reassurance, you are supporting your partner in retraining their mind. You are showing that discomfort, doubt, and unanswered questions are not emergencies – that they can be borne without anything bad happening. However small or even meaningless these moments might seem at the time, they are strong acts of learning that gradually loosen the strength anxiety has in your lives.

There is no recovery without acts of courage. Not doing a compulsion, sitting with feelings, allowing a question to go unanswered - these are not passive acts. They are deliberate steps toward recovery. Long-term freedom cannot exist without them. Every step builds a solid foundation in resilience, trust, and self-belief over time. Maybe that thing you've just done doesn't look like much, perhaps it's not dramatic, but every time you sit with uncertainty, you're making something real.

10.5 Restoring joy and connection

Recovery can quietly turn into another full-time job where every move is monitored for improvement. This commitment does matter, and so does consistency, but let's not forget that healing doesn't just come down to effort and endurance. Joy is deeply therapeutic. Allowing some pleasure, play, and connection into your lives helps rewire a relationship that ROCD usually pushes toward seriousness and strain.

As you know, ROCD strains a relationship until it has successfully removed all pleasure, narrowing the scope to doubt, fear, and analysis. Deliberately creating rituals that nourish your bond can serve as a strong counterbalance to stress. They don't have to be grand or pushed. Simple, steady times of bonding - meals shared without screens, a daily walk, coffee time, a favourite movie, or even

Uncertainty is the heartbeat of OCD - and learning to live with it is at the heart of recovery.

just a fun game night - show both of you that there is much more to your relationship than just signs and healing steps. These rituals bring regularity and security, and also let fun and comfort back in.

10.6 Tracking progress and setbacks

Keeping a journal, not to list symptoms, analyse thoughts or log every tough moment, but to notice and write down growth, can be a quietly strong practice. This record becomes a place where you can note down those things that might otherwise be missed: when your partner fought off a compulsion, when you held a boundary with love and kindness, when you shared laughs and warmth, even on days that seem sad or disappointing.

They don't have to be long. They don't have to be eloquent. One sentence is enough - a single line marking strength, marking resilience. Eventually, this record turns into proof of changes that anxiety will want to try to dismiss or minimise. When setbacks come, as they always do on the journey toward recovery, looking back over these pages helps fight off the internal narrative that might say, "nothing is working" or "we're back at the beginning." Let your journal speak of how far you've already come, how much strength you've built and how many difficult moments you have already survived together.

10.7 Knowing when to reach out

Self-help is powerful, but it's not meant to replace therapy. If anxiety is unmanageable or if you are both exhausted, reaching out to a professional for OCD is an act of wisdom, not defeat.

Exposure and Response Prevention (ERP), Acceptance and Commitment Therapy (ACT), Cognitive Behaviour Therapy (CBT), Mindfulness Practice, and Psychoeducation are highly effective for ROCD. You can also ask about couples-based approaches, where both partners learn skills together. If you need individual therapy as a partner (which I find is most common), then take it. That's part of your own recovery roadmap.

Joy strengthens the bond that ROCD tries to weaken.

10.8 Making peace with the journey

As a partner, you may come to realise that supporting someone through ROCD is never about "curing" the disorder or erasing every intrusive thought.

Recovery is about building a life that is bigger, fuller, and richer than the anxiety itself. For you, this often means letting go of the urge to control, fix, or rescue, and instead approaching each day with patience, presence, and steady, compassionate support.

You do not wait for the moment when doubt goes away, or when compulsions stop. You start living fully with your partner, allowing uncertainty to coexist with love and connection. There is fear, there is doubt, and there is discomfort - let it be. It does not define what love or life is shared.

Real growth happens in those little, often silent moments: when you share your feelings honestly, when you work through anxiety together, or when you sit with each other in discomfort.

Speaking words like, *"We can handle uncertainty. We can love through fear. We can choose peace even in the mess,"* is not just saying - it is doing, and it is resilience.

Self-compassion for yourself and your partner is essential throughout this process, and by now you probably recognise what I said at the beginning. It really is an essential ingredient towards recovery. Self-compassion honours your own limits, respects your own feelings, and remembers that supporting someone with ROCD is a journey, not a quick fix. Letting go of control creates space for both of you to grow individually and together, without allowing the disorder to dominate your relationship.

This journey is about observing the swings, taking note of acts of bravery, and striving to keep a life of love, connection, and happiness notwithstanding the return of doubt. In embracing this approach, recovery work becomes an agent not only of healing from ROCD but also of re-establishing and nourishing the relationship.

Journaling moments of progress helps you notice evidence of growth, even when the journey feels uncertain.

10.9 Renewing Hope

Now and then, it can be grounding to pause and remember why you began this journey together

In the daily struggles of supporting a person with ROCD, doubt, fear, and the need for healing can easily be fuelled. Taking time to reflect on your "why" can help you remember the love, promise, and shared values that brought both of you together from the very beginning.

Read old journal entries or notes exchanged during better days, look at photos that can recall happy moments, or write a new note to each other, sharing what you appreciate. Such small acts of reflection and recognition will create pockets of warmth and reassurance, thereby reinforcing the emotional connection that ROCD has strained.

Hope does not have to be loud. It is most times silent - a soft and gentle confidence that the relationship and the two of you are worth fighting for. This is what brings you both to the realisation that getting better should not be an individualistic pursuit of fighting off the demons of anxiety, but rather a way to feed your connection: finding the good that already exists and carrying that shared purpose forward, even on a difficult day.

Recovery is not a place you get to once and for all. It's a way of walking together, day by day, with some days rocky, uncertain, or exhausting, and others smooth and more sure. With every step, both of you are learning how to live, how to love, and how to sit with so much uncertainty.

Acts of love are the care and willingness to stay with an open heart in the face of fear. Such love builds safety and connection and resilience between you and your partner, even if sometimes it seems like things are not moving on or the anxiety is very high.

You might never know just how much what you do means to your partner, but it does matter a lot more than you can ever imagine. Every

Personal therapy is a sign of strength, not defeat.

word spoken kindly, every moment shared, and every boundary held with compassion are building blocks for trust, stability, and growth.

Remember, loving with ROCD does not make the love any less. It just asks for a different kind of strength - yours and your partner's - and every single step that you take together is a show of that strength.

***We've weathered storms before.
We'll do it again.***

Chapter 11

Love that Learns

Final Reflections

When you reach this point in your journey, you've probably learned something that isn't printed in any manual. Recovery isn't just about the one who has ROCD, it's about both of you learning to live gently, more consciously and more courageously in the presence of uncertainty.

This final chapter is a space to pause, breathe, and notice what's changed – inside you, inside your relationship, and in the quiet rhythm of your shared life.

11.1 Re-discovering Connection and Resilience

You may have imagined love as something that fixes, rescues or heals when you first started caring for your partner through ROCD. Over time, you've probably discovered that love doesn't always fix. It learns to sit beside pain without turning away. It stops asking *"How can I make this go away?"* and starts asking *"How can we hold this together?"*

That is where the fundamental transformation happens for the two of you.

11.2 Your Hidden Gem

It's hard to see it when you're in the middle of fear and repetition, and many partners/carers say that, despite that pain, this learning experience has deepened their capacity for patience, self-awareness and love. They've found a way to set boundaries with compassion and to trust that peace can return, even in chaos. That's not romanticising a struggle – it's recognising growth.

11.3 Re-discovering yourself

It's now your time to look inward again. For so long, your focus has been outward, either on your partner, their fears or their progress. You are more than their partner or carer. You are a person with dreams, needs, and passions that deserve to be alive and tended to.

In a Quiet Moment:

Ask yourself gently:

- *"What have I learned about myself through this?"*
- *"What parts of me have I rediscovered or want to reclaim?"*
- *"How can I build a life that not only honours love, but also independence?"*

These questions don't take you away from your partner – they bring you back to yourself, which in turn brings new energy to the relationship.

11.4 Shared Resilience

Resilience doesn't mean you never falter. It means you return, again and again, to the values that matter most to you – like kindness, hope, honesty and connection.

Together, you can learn that storms do indeed pass, even when that fear feels endless; it does shift.

You've built a relationship strong enough to hold uncertainty without breaking.

That's resilience in its truest form, based on flexibility and not invincibility.

11.5 The Language of Healing

Healing is made of simple words, spoken freely, so as you move forward, remember to talk them often:

- *"I love you".*
- *"I'm here".*
- *"This is hard, but we'll get through It".*
- *"Let's take this one moment at a time".*

These phrases can be steady reminders in the background of recovery, reminders that connection is the antidote to fear.

11.6 When the Road Feels Long Again

Old patterns may still return, reassurance may sneak back, and anxiety may fill the room. This does not mean you are failing. It means you are human, and when those moments come, do what you've already done so far – pause, breathe and return to what you've learned.

11.7 Choosing Hope Over Searching for Certainty

The human mind often craves certainty, but life rarely provides it, especially in areas such as relationships, health, identity, and the future.

Certainty is often an illusion, and we can tend to believe that *if we think enough, research enough, or analyse enough*, then we'll finally feel settled. In reality, most of life's important questions don't have final answers, and the search for such can become endless and exhausting, creating anxiety rather than relief.

Hope allows you to move forward without having all the answers. In Chapter 10, I described hope as a soft, steady confidence that the relationship and the two of you are worth fighting for. Certainty feeds fear, whilst hope feeds resilience. When we search for certainty, we're usually trying to eliminate fear. Ironically, this often makes fear strong because every new doubt feels threatening.

Hope doesn't promise safety but builds emotional flexibility. It says, *"Even if things are unclear, I can cope."* That belief is far more stabilising than certainty.

Certainty collapses under stress, so when life throws something unexpected like illness, loss or change, then certainty breaks. Hope, on the other hand, adapts. It allows room for change, growth and new meanings to emerge over time.

Hope restores trust in yourself as searching for certainty often implies *"I can't cope unless I know"*, whereas hope says *"I trust myself to respond, whatever happens"*.

That shift builds self-trust, confidence and emotional safety, which is especially important when living with chronic stress, pain or uncertainty.

Hope keeps life's doors open, creating possibility, learning, surprise and connection. Certainty closes doors because it implies that it can only turn out one way.

I could go on, but I think you've got my drift – certainty promises comfort. Still, it delivers anxiety and choosing hope is courageous and a decision to live life fully without waiting for perfect answers.

A Few Closing Words

I hope this gives you a clear roadmap moving forward, that's full of compassion, connection, courage and choice.

You have found out that peace is not a place to reach but something you make, one soft moment after another.

Thank you for staying the course and reading my book. I know caring for a partner with ROCD is not easy, but it's deeply meaningful. You are learning to love, not because everything is easy but because you are choosing presence over perfection and connection over chaos.

The love you give, the boundaries you hold, the self-care you practice – these all matter deeply and are part of a healing story that is still unfolding.

As you close this book (or return to it when needed), remember ROCD does not define you and your partner. You are greater than it, and every step you take together builds a life that proves that.

I wish you success, hope and happiness moving forward.

Best wishes

Tracy

Glossary of Common OCD-Related Terms

This glossary is offered with care. You do not need to relate to every term for it to be relevant to you. Some words may feel close to home; others may not. Take what helps, skip what doesn't, and remember that experiencing OCD, or learning about it, does not require you to fit any definition perfectly.

This glossary is intended to support understanding, not labels. OCD looks and feels different for each person, but the terms below reflect common experiences.

Obsessive Compulsive Disorder (OCD)

A mental health condition in which a person experiences unwanted, intrusive thoughts and feels compelled to repeat actions or mental rituals to reduce distress. OCD is not a personality trait, preference, or habit, and it can be exhausting and deeply distressing.

Obsessions

Unwanted thoughts, images, or urges that repeatedly intrude on the mind and cause anxiety, fear, or discomfort. These thoughts are not chosen and do not reflect a person's character or intentions.

Compulsions

Actions or mental rituals are performed to try to relieve the anxiety caused by obsessions. Relief is usually brief, which can trap the person in a painful cycle.

Intrusive Thoughts

Sudden, involuntary thoughts or images that feel disturbing or upsetting. Many people experience intrusive thoughts, but in OCD, they are especially sticky and distressing. Having them does not mean a person wants them or will act on them.

Anxiety

The intense fear, unease, or sense that something is "wrong" that often accompanies OCD thoughts and drives compulsive behaviour.

Reassurance Seeking

Repeatedly asking others, or yourself, for confirmation, comfort, or certainty (for example, asking if a relationship is normal or repeatedly checking your own feelings). While this may bring momentary relief, it often strengthens OCD over time.

Checking

A common compulsion involving repeatedly verifying things, such as locks, appliances, messages, or memories, to feel safe or certain.

Contamination OCD

A form of OCD centred on fears of germs, illness, dirt, or toxins, often leading to excessive cleaning, washing, or avoidance. This goes far beyond ordinary concerns about hygiene.

Harm OCD

(sometimes described more gently as "fear-of-harm thoughts")

OCD involves intrusive fears about causing harm to oneself or others. These thoughts are especially distressing because they go against the person's values and desires.

Relationship OCD (ROCD)

A form of OCD focused on doubts, fears, or intrusive thoughts about romantic or other relationships. These doubts feel urgent and distressing, even when the relationship itself is healthy or meaningful.

Relationship-Focused Intrusive Thoughts

Unwanted thoughts about whether you genuinely love your partner, whether the relationship is "right," or whether you should leave. These thoughts are driven by anxiety, not by hidden truths.

Partner-Focused ROCD

A pattern of OCD where attention becomes fixated on a partner's perceived flaws, habits, or traits, leading to constant comparison, analysis, or doubt.

Pure O (Primarily Obsessional OCD) *(some people prefer "mostly mental compulsions")*

A presentation of OCD where compulsions are mostly internal rather than visible, such as mental reviewing, reassurance in your own mind, or trying to "figure out" thoughts.

Rumination

Getting stuck in repetitive, circular thinking to find certainty, meaning, or relief. In OCD, rumination functions as a mental compulsion.

Comparing

Mentally comparing your relationship or partner to others, past relationships, or imagined "ideal" relationships in an attempt to gain certainty. This often increases doubt rather than resolving it.

Avoidance

Deliberately staying away from people, places, objects, or situations that trigger OCD anxiety. In ROCD, this can include avoiding commitment, affection, or conversations about the future. While understandable, avoidance can shrink a person's world over time.

Magical Thinking

The belief that specific thoughts, words, or actions can prevent harm or cause events, even when there is no logical connection. This can feel very real to the person experiencing it.

Mental Compulsions

Internal rituals such as counting, praying, repeating phrases, reviewing memories, or neutralising thoughts to reduce distress.

ERP (Exposure and Response Prevention)

A well-established, evidence-based therapy for OCD that involves gradually facing feared thoughts or situations while learning not to perform compulsions.

Tolerance of Uncertainty

Learning to live with doubt and discomfort without trying to eliminate it. Building tolerance for uncertainty is a key part of OCD recovery.

Insight

The extent to which a person recognises that OCD thoughts and urges may be exaggerated or unreasonable, even when they still feel powerful and distressing.

Triggers

Situations, sensations, or thoughts that intensify OCD symptoms. Triggers can be external or internal.

Stigma

Misunderstandings and stereotypes about OCD that minimise its seriousness or misrepresent it often make it harder for people to feel understood or seek help.

EgoDystonic *(a clinical term; often experienced simply as "this doesn't feel like me")*

A term meaning the thoughts feel foreign, unwanted, and deeply against a person's values. This is common in OCD and often a major source of distress.

A note on clinical language

Some terms in this glossary come from clinical or academic settings and may feel heavy, technical, or impersonal. In recovery-focused or everyday conversations, people often use gentler language instead.

You may see or hear the following expressed in softer ways:

- **Egodystonic** → *"These thoughts don't feel like me"*.
- **Compulsions** → *"safety behaviours" or "things I do to cope"*.
- **Reassurance seeking** → *"needing certainty or comfort"*.
- **Exposure and Response Prevention (ERP)** → *"learning to face fears without rituals"*.
- **Tolerance of uncertainty** → *"learning to live with not knowing"*.

Clinical language can be helpful for diagnosis and treatment, but it is not a requirement for healing. What matters most is finding words that feel supportive, humane, and true to your own experience.

Additional notes on Relationship OCD language

In Relationship OCD, everyday experiences such as normal doubts, changing feelings, or noticing a partner's flaws can become magnified and frightening. OCD turns these everyday human experiences into urgent questions that feel impossible to ignore.

Language around relationships is especially sensitive. Many people with ROCD fear that having doubts means something is fundamentally wrong. OCD feeds on the desire for certainty and reassurance, not on the quality of the relationship itself.

As with all OCD themes, the goal is not to eliminate doubts, but to learn how to live without constantly interrogating them.

References & Resources

Kobori, O., Salkovskis, P. M., Read, J., Lounes, N., & Wong, A. (2017). *A qualitative study of the investigation of reassurance seeking in obsessive–compulsive disorder: Carers' experiences of reassurance provision. The Cognitive Behaviour Therapist, 10,* e10.

Stein, D. J., Costa, D. L. C., Lochner, C., Miguel, E. C., Reddy, Y. C. J., Shavitt, R. G., van den Heuvel, O. A., & Simpson, H. B. (2019). *Obsessive–compulsive disorder.* Nature Reviews Disease Primers, 5(52). https://doi.org/10.1038/s41572-019-0102-3

Neff, K. (2011). *Selfcompassion: The proven power of being kind to yourself* (1st ed.). William Morrow.

Figley, C. R. (1995). *Compassion fatigue: Coping with secondary traumatic stress disorder in those who treat the traumatized.* Brunner/Mazel.

Maslach, C., & Leiter, M. P. (2016). *Burnout: A brief history and how to reverse it.* Harvard Business Review Press.

OCD in Brief - OCD Action. https://ocdaction.org.uk/learn-about-ocd/ocd-in-brief/

Albert U, Baffa A, Maina G. Family accommodation in adult obsessive-compulsive disorder: clinical perspectives. Psychol Res Behav Manag. 2017 Sep 20;10:293-304. doi: 10.2147/PRBM.S124359. PMID: 29033617; PMCID: PMC5614765.

Setting Healthy Boundaries in Relationships: Examples, Tips, and Strat. https://shararat.in/blogs/relationshipintimacy/setting-healthy-boundaries-in-relationships-examples-tips-and-strategies

Olatunji, B. O., Davis, M. L., Powers, M. B., & Smits, J. A. J. (2013). Cognitive-behavioral therapy for obsessive-compulsive disorder: A meta-analysis of treatment outcome and moderators. *Journal of Psychiatric Research*, 47(1), 33–41. https://doi.org/10.1016/j.jpsychires.2012.08.020. PubMed

Öst, L.-G., Havnen, A., Hansen, B., & Kvale, G. (2015). Cognitive-behavioral treatments of obsessive-compulsive disorder: A systematic review and meta-analysis of studies published 1993–2014. *Clinical Psychology Review*, 40, 156–169. https://doi.org/10.1016/j.cpr.2015.06.003. PubMed

Soondrum, T., Wang, X., Gao, F., Liu, Q., Fan, J., & Zhu, X. (2022). The applicability of Acceptance and Commitment Therapy for obsessive-compulsive disorder: A systematic review and meta-analysis. Brain Sciences, 12(5), 656. https://doi.org/10.3390/brainsci12050656. MDPI+1

Riquelme-Marín, A., Rosa-Alcázar, A. I., & Ortigosa-Quiles, J. M. (2022). Mindfulness-based psychotherapy in patients with obsessive-compulsive disorder: A meta-analytical study. *International Journal of Clinical and Health Psychology*, 22(3), Article 100321. https://doi.org/10.1016/j.ijchp.2022.100321. PubMed+1

Bluett, E. J., Homan, K. J., Morrison, K. L., Levin, M. E., & Twohig, M. P. (2014). Acceptance and commitment therapy for anxiety and OCD-spectrum disorders: An empirical review. *Journal of Anxiety Disorders*, 28(6), 612–624. https://doi.org/10.1016/j.janxdis.2014.06.008. PubMed

Foa, E. B., Yadin, E., & Lichner, T. K. (2012). *Exposure and response (ritual) prevention for obsessive-compulsive disorder: Therapist guide* (2nd ed.). Oxford University Press. Oxford University Press+1

Koran, L. M., Hanna, G. L., Hollander, E., Nestadt, G., Simpson, H. B., & American Psychiatric Association Work Group on Obsessive-Compulsive Disorder. (2007). Practice guideline for the treatment of patients with obsessive-compulsive disorder. *American Journal of Psychiatry*, 164(7 Suppl), 5–53. https://pubmed.ncbi.nlm.nih.gov/17849776/ . PubMed

National Institute for Health and Care Excellence. (2005). Obsessive-compulsive disorder: Core interventions in the treatment of obsessive-compulsive disorder and body dysmorphic disorder (NICE Clinical Guideline No. CG31). https://www.nice.org.uk/guidance/cg31

Soondrum, T., Wang, X., Gao, F., Liu, Q., Fan, J., & Zhu, X. (2022). *The applicability of Acceptance and Commitment Therapy for obsessivecompulsive disorder: A systematic review and metaanalysis.* **Brain Sciences**, **12**(5), 656. https://doi.org/10.3390/brainsci12050656

RiquelmeMarín, A., RosaAlcázar, A. I., & OrtigosaQuiles, J. M. (2022). *Mindfulnessbased psychotherapy in patients with obsessive–compulsive disorder: A metaanalytical study.* **International Journal of Clinical and Health Psychology**, 22(3), 100321. https://doi.org/10.1016/j.ijchp.2022.100321

Olatunji, B. O., Davis, M. L., Powers, M. B., & Smits, J. A. J. (2013). *Cognitive-behavioral therapy for obsessivecompulsive disorder: A meta-analysis of treatment outcome and moderators.* **Journal of Anxiety Disorders**, 27(5), 471–482. https://doi.org/10.1016/j.janxdis.2013.05.004

Twohig, M. P., & Crosby, J. M. (2014). *Acceptance and Commitment Therapy for anxiety and OCDspectrum disorders: An empirical review.* **Journal of Anxiety Disorders, 28**(6), 612–624. https://doi.org/10.1016/j.janxdis.2014.05.007

Fisher, P. L., & Wells, A. (2005). *How effective is cognitive behaviour therapy for obsessive–compulsive disorder? A clinical and methodological review*. **Psychological Medicine**, 35(4), 574–587. https://doi.org/10.1017/S0033291704003839

Haller, H., Breilmann, P., Schröter, M., Dobos, G., & Cramer, H. (2021). *A systematic review and metaanalysis of acceptance- and mindfulness-based interventions for DSM5 anxiety disorders.* **Scientific Reports, 11**, 20385. https://doi.org/10.1038/s41598-021-99882-w

(International OCD Foundation. (n.d.). *Exposure and response prevention therapy.* https://iocdf.org/ocd-treatment-guide/exposure-response-prevention/)

Neff, K. (n.d.). *Exercise 2: Self-Compassion Break.* Self-Compassion. https://self-compassion.org/exercises/exercise-2-self-compassion-break/

Bowlby, J. (1969). *Attachment and loss: Volume I. Attachment.* Basic Books.

Ainsworth, M. D. S., Blehar, M. C., Waters, E., & Wall, S. (1978). *Patterns of attachment: A psychological study of the Strange Situation.* Lawrence Erlbaum Associates.

Abramowitz, J. S., McKay, D., & Taylor, S. (2012). Clinical handbook of obsessive-compulsive disorder and related problems. Johns Hopkins University Press.

Abramowitz, J. S., & Jacoby, R. J. (2015). Obsessive–compulsive disorder in adults. In J. D. Wright (Ed.), International encyclopedia of the social & behavioral sciences (2nd ed., pp. 41–46). Elsevier.

Salkovskis, P. M., Shafran, R., Rachman, S., & Freeston, M. H. (1999). Multiple pathways to inflated responsibility beliefs in obsessional problems: Possible origins and implications for therapy and research. Behaviour Research and Therapy, 37(11), 1055–1072.

Other References to be read in conjunction with Chapter 5

Strategies for a Recovery-Friendly Environment

- Psychoeducation for Loved Ones and Self: Educating partners or family members about ROCD — how intrusive thoughts work, and why reassurance or helping with compulsions actually reinforces OCD — reduces misunderstandings and prevents enabling behaviours (Olatunji et al., 2013).
- Reducing Accommodation and Reassurance-Seeking: Loved ones can support recovery by avoiding giving reassurance, participating in mental checking, or helping avoid triggers. Instead, they can offer calm presence, empathy, and encouragement for using coping strategies or ERP exercises (Fisher & Wells, 2005; Soondrum et al., 2022).
- Establishing Predictable Routines and Boundaries: Consistent daily routines and agreed-upon boundaries (for example, designated "no-doubt discussions" times) help reduce the uncertainty and instability that often fuel ROCD, providing a steady backdrop for therapy and coping (Haller et al., 2021).
- Creating Safe and Calm Spaces: Physical and emotional spaces where compulsions aren't allowed — such as "OCD-free zones" or times for hobbies and self-care — support emotional regulation and provide a safe environment for exposure practices (RiquelmeMarín et al., 2022).
- Encouraging Mindfulness, Acceptance, and Values-Led Behavior: Practicing mindfulness (observing thoughts without reacting) and focusing on personal values (such as kindness, honesty, or connection) helps individuals tolerate uncertainty without compulsions (Twohig & Crosby, 2014; Haller et al., 2021).

- Support Networks and Social Connection: Maintaining friendships, hobbies, or support groups outside the relationship strengthens resilience and helps reduce compulsive dependence on reassurance from the partner (Soondrum et al., 2022).
- Normalizing Discomfort and Reducing Shame: Approaching doubts or uncertainty as part of ROCD, rather than personal failure, fosters self-compassion and reduces shame, which can otherwise exacerbate compulsive behaviours (Twohig & Crosby, 2014).
- Self-Care and Stress Management: Healthy sleep, gentle exercise, nutrition, and relaxation routines help reduce overall anxiety, making it easier to tolerate discomfort and engage in therapy (Haller et al., 2021).

Resources

International OCD Foundations (IOCDF) – iocdf.org – excellent for carers, sufferers, support groups and webinars.

OCD UK – ocduk.org – a UK based charity with family resources, forums and guidance.

Online peer support communities: many local and international Facebook groups or forms focused on ROCD and carers supporting someone with OCD.

OCD Action – ocdaction.org.uk – support groups, action lines, webinars.

www.ingramcontent.com/pod-product-compliance
Ingram Content Group UK Ltd.
Pitfield, Milton Keynes, MK11 3LW, UK
UKHW040232290926
15471UKWH00002B/147

9 781807 230760